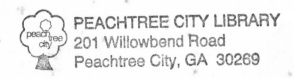

INDIRA GANDHI

NAYANA CURRIMBHOY

INDIRA GANDHI

FRANKLIN WATTS
NEW YORK I LONDON I TORONTO I SYDNEY I 1985
AN IMPACT BIOGRAPHY

A GROLIER COMPANY

UPI/Bettmann Newsphotos: pp. 7 (top and bottom), 33, 38, 48, 53, 62, 68, 72, 79, 86, 92, 106; AP/Wide World Photos: pp. 27, 98.

Map by Vantage Art, Inc.

Library of Congress Cataloging in Publication Data

Currimbhoy, Nayana.
Indira Gandhi.

(An Impact biography)
Bibliography: p.
Includes index.
Summary: Presents the life of the prime minister of India from her lonely childhood though her rise to power.
1. Gandhi, Indira, 1917–   —Juvenile literature.
2. India—Politics and government—1947–   —Juvenile literature. 3. Prime ministers—India—Biography—Juvenile literature. [1. Gandhi, Indira, 1917–
2. Prime ministers. 3. India—Politics and government —20th century] I. Title.
DS481.G23S235   1985   954.04′5′0924[B][92]   85-10506
ISBN 0-531-10064-2

CONTENTS

TO TARIK

INDIRA GANDHI

How hard it is to keep from being king,
when it's in you, and in the situation

Robert Frost
(quoted by Indira Gandhi
in a letter to her
son, Rajiv Gandhi)

THE
ASSASSINATION

1

It was the last day of October 1984, and the cool, clear morning held the promise of a balmy day. Mrs. Indira Gandhi, prime minister of India, adjusted the folds of her orange sari, asked an aide if she looked all right, and set out to walk the one hundred yards that separated her home from her office. It was just after 9:00 A.M. and Mrs. Gandhi had an interview with actor-director Peter Ustinov, for a television serial.

The graveled path separating the two buildings could be traveled by car, but Mrs. Gandhi preferred to walk. She walked alone, followed at a discreet distance by aides and bodyguards. Halfway along the path, under an arching bougainvillea vine, two security guards, Beant Singh and Satwant Singh, stood to attention on either side of the road. As Mrs. Gandhi walked toward them, Satwant Singh raised his Sten gun in what, for one mistaken moment, her bodyguard thought was a salute. After that, things went completely out of control.

Beant Singh, who was less than three feet away from Mrs. Gandhi, pulled out his .38 revolver and fired five shots at her in quick succession, while Satwant Singh pumped fourteen rounds from his Sten gun into her body. "What are you doing?" cried Mrs. Gandhi in her final moment of clarity, before she crumpled to the ground, bleeding. Her body was riddled with sixteen bullets, at least eleven of which had pierced her chest and stomach. Although she was rushed immediately to the hospital by shaken aides and relatives, she was dead when she arrived, one more world leader to be killed by an assassin's bullet.

Indira Priyadarshini Nehru Gandhi was born to politics the way some people are born to money or social position. Both her grandfather Motilal Nehru and her father Jawaharlal Nehru played prominent roles in India's struggle against British colonial rule, and Indira's home in the city of Allahabad was the hub of India's freedom movement. "I think I attended my first political meeting when I was three," she recalled later.

Jawaharlal Nehru became independent India's first prime minister. Then, in 1966, two years after his death, Mrs. Gandhi—who had been her father's hostess and close confidant—was chosen to lead the world's most populous democracy. For almost two decades this small, autocratic woman with her charming smile and her white-streaked hair ruled India with a dominance that has few parallels in democratic history. With her uncanny political instinct and her almost intuitive understanding of her people, she dwarfed all opposition. She could be warm and considerate, but she could also be completely ruthless. She was charismatic and she was shrewd, but her critics have accused her of playing the politics of expediency. She would do anything, they said, to stay in power.

She led India into the nuclear age in 1974, when Indian scientists exploded an underground nuclear device in the desert of Rajasthan. In 1980 she saw her nation into the space age, when it launched its own satellites on its own rocket. Mostly due to her adroit maneuvering, India became a leader of the Third World and a dominant power in South Asia. However, Mrs. Gandhi has also been held largely responsible for the sorry state of Indian politics. Known as the "giant killer" because she broke the power of every politician who did not derive his influence directly from her, Mrs. Gandhi encouraged sycophants, or flatterers, around her. Worse, she alternately suppressed and encouraged the bickering between India's various states and communities according to her needs, a fact that has become the bane of politics in this complex country.

And so it happened that when she died, a few days before her sixty-seventh birthday, Mrs. Gandhi's death occurred in the manner in which she had lived: in the public eye, and shrouded in controversy.

Both her killers were Sikhs, members of an independent religious sect with a proud militant tradition, whose home is the northwestern state of Punjab. The Sikh religion dictates that members never cut their hair; so the Sikh men, with their full beards and colorful turbans with which they cover their hair, are a highly visible community. Although they form only 2 percent of the Indian population, their determination and resourcefulness have led the Sikhs to play an important role in the country's life. For the past few years, however, an extremist faction of the sect has been agitating for a separate Sikh nation called Khalistan, or "land of the pure." The situation came to a head in 1984 when Sikh extremists turned their most holy shrine, the Golden Temple, into a heavily armed fortress. From the temple, which sits beside a lake in the Punjabi city of Amritsar, the rebels threatened to terrorize the nation, murdering and looting at will.

In June, after failing to come to a peaceful settlement with the Sikhs, Mrs. Gandhi sent the army to flush out the temple. More than six hundred people, including the extremist leader Sant Jarnail Singh Bhindranwale, were killed in the battle that followed. It was a bold step, but one that enraged

Sikh feelings ever further. It was a step that cost Mrs. Gandhi her life. Her two assassins, when they were satisfied that she was dead, threw down their guns and raised their arms in surrender. "We have done what we had to do. Now you do what you have to do," said twenty-one-year-old Satwant Singh.

Outside the hospital, where doctors had put her on heart and kidney machines in a desperate effort to revive her, crowds gathered, numbed and disbelieving. Throughout the country, rumors ran rampant. There was only one terse news announcement in the morning, stating that Mrs. Gandhi had been wounded by bullets, and then there was silence. The state-owned radio continued to play Hindi film songs, and everywhere people gathered in knots, wondering if the prime minister was really dead. Most of them believed that she would survive, simply because it seemed impossible to imagine an India without Indira. At 1:45 P.M. the state-controlled press agency finally sent the bulletin: Mrs. Gandhi is dead.

In the days that followed, fires of vengeance burned in Delhi and neighboring towns in northern India, as hysterical bands attacked Sikhs, burned their beards, and destroyed their shops and homes. "Blood for blood," the attackers cried. The death toll passed a thousand, and the army was

A gun carriage draped with flowers bears the body of Indira Gandhi as the funeral procession moves through the streets of New Delhi on its way to the Yamuna River for the cremation ceremony on November 3, 1984. Rajiv (second from left), with his wife and daughter, stands beside his mother's funeral pyre.

called out to control the mob that threatened to be the worst in the thirty-seven-year-old history of independent India.

Delhi seemed to be the worst hit by the violence. Tanks moved into the city and the army patrolled, as carcasses of tires and cars smoldered in streets strewn with debris, sending columns of smoke far into the distance. It seemed as though the entire city was burning.

At the same time, Delhi was a picture of decorum, dignity, and pageantry as the country—and the world—paid its last respects to Indira Gandhi. Leaders and heads of state of over a hundred nations, as well as mourners from all over the country, poured into the capital. For two days, Mrs. Gandhi's body lay in state at the house that used to be her father's official residence, Teen Murti. Then, on Saturday afternoon, her body, draped in the Indian tricolor and covered with flowers, was taken in a gun carriage to the banks of the holy Yamuna River. There, in keeping with the Hindu tradition of cremation, it was placed on a bed of teak and sandalwood and set aflame by her son, Rajiv. "Indira will live forever," shouted the crowds. "As long as the sun and moon exist, Indira your name will remain." Her family stood, silent, beside the funeral pyre, while white-clad friends, relatives, and wellwishers walked slowly around the fire, folding their hands in the Hindu salute that is a greeting as well as a farewell.

Indira Gandhi's hold on the Indian imagination was remarkable. She had become a household word, and her face—with its patrician nose and its black, hooded eyes—was recognized even in the remotest of India's small, sleepy villages.

Her political impact was equally remarkable. For eighteen years, India's politics had polarized into two basic forces: pro-Indira and anti-Indira, with even the opposition parties taking their stance and strategy from her. The day after her death, The Indian Express editorialized, "both our politics and our political debates have centered around her.

We have been for her, or against her. Either way, we have been mesmerized by her."

For her part, Mrs. Gandhi's entire life was linked with Indian politics. Toward the end of her life, like the kings and queens of old, she began to believe that she, and her children, were born to rule India. Over the years, Indira Gandhi had come to identify her destiny with that of the country. "If I die today," she said in her last public speech, just the day before she died, "every drop of my blood will invigorate the nation."

ANCIENT CULTURE, YOUNG DEMOCRACY

2

Thousands of years ago, India's Hindu sages meditating on the nature of the universe concluded that there were many different realities, and that they all existed at the same time. This is one of the fundamental beliefs of Hindu philosophy. And it offers a useful way of understanding the complex, multilayered society that Indira Gandhi ruled. More than anything else, India today is the land of many realities.

In villages tucked away in remote mountain valleys, time is still measured by the passing of seasons, and the world is still bordered by the village that lies a day's walk away. In cities like Bombay, meanwhile, rich men buy clothes from Paris and eat ice cream flown in from Manila, and scientists succeed in making a rocket that reaches the moon.

In the north, the Himalayan mountain range straddles the Indian subcontinent like a giant roof, protecting it from invasions and from the biting winter winds of central Asia. The Himalayas—many of whose snow-covered peaks have never been climbed—form a barrier that is one hundred to two hundred miles deep and about twenty thousand feet high. Medieval tribes, tempted by the great wealth of India's central plains, were forced to face treacherous mountain crossings in order to enter the country. As a result, the conquering tribes came only in small numbers, and were not able to destroy the existing cultures. Instead, they made room for themselves within the society.

South of the mountains lies a great, fertile plain that stretches almost across the entire breadth of Northern India. Dotted today with tight clusters of mud huts and small patchwork-quilt fields, this plain was the cradle of one of the world's earliest civilizations and the birthplace of two major world religions—Buddhism and Hinduism. Waves of conquering tribes ruled the plain for a while and then were gradually absorbed into the mainstream of Indian civilization.

Southern India is a peninsula, bordered by the Arabian Sea to the west and the Bay of Bengal to the east. The long coastal strips on either side have many natural ports. From these ports ancient mariners sailed to Sumer in the valley of the Euphrates River, hugging the dangerous Persian coastline and using for a compass a crow that would fly to the nearest point of land when it was released. Except for a narrow coastal belt on either side, the Indian peninsula is an immense tableland known as the Deccan Plateau. A band of hills separates the plateau from the great plain, acting as a natural barrier that has served to prevent the rulers of the North from overtaking the South. As a result, the history and culture of Southern India have run a different course from those of the North.

This vast country with its dramatically different physical features is united, in a sense, by its climate. For nine months of the year, the wind blows from the north, dropping its moisture on the snowy peaks of the Himalayas before it reaches the subcontinent. For these nine months, there is no rain in India. Then, in June, from the southwest come the monsoon winds, blowing over the Indian Ocean, bringing rain to the subcontinent.

MONGOLIA

U.S.S.R.

IRAN

AFGHANISTAN

CHINA

PAKISTAN

JAMMU
AND KASHMIR

HIMACHAL PRADESH

Amritsar

PUNJAB

HARYANA

GREAT INDIAN
DESERT

Delhi

New Delhi

Jaipur

RAJASTHAN

UTTAR
PRADESH

H I M A L A Y A S

NEPAL

SIKKIM

ARUNCHAL PRADESH
(terr.)

BHUTAN

Darjeeling

ASSAM

NAGALAND

MEGHALAYA

MANIPUR

Lucknow

Kanpur

Allahabad

Varanasi

Ganges River

BANGLA-
DESH

TRIPURA

GUJARAT

Ahmadabad

MADHYA PRADESH

Indore

Bhopal

Jabalpur

BIHAR

WEST
BENGAL

Howrah

Calcutta

BURMA

Nagpur

ORISSA

MAHARASHTRA

Bombay

Arabian Sea

DECCAN PLATEAU

Hyderabad

ANDHRA
PRADESH

Bay of Bengal

KARNATAKA

Laccadive Sea

Bangalore

Madras

LACCADIVE ISLANDS

TAMIL NADU

Coimbatore

KERALA

Madurai

SRI LANKA

Indian Ocean

INDIA

Every year—after the hot, dry months, when the temperature reaches 120°F in the northern plains—the country awaits the coming of the rains. For three months, the countryside turns lush and green. Storms and thundershowers are common, and the sky is always overcast. In a country where 70 percent of the people are farmers, the entire economy is dependent upon the monsoon rains. But the monsoon can be destructive to the land. Sometimes it rains too little, and crops and cattle droop and die. Sometimes it rains too much, and angry, swollen rivers overflow their banks, sweeping away entire villages.

There are more people in India than in the Soviet Union and the United States put together. But there is almost no uniformity of character, style, food, or dress among India's seven hundred million people. The contrasts and contradictions of Indian life can be explained on three levels.

Most apparent are the regional differences. Each region in the country has its own history, going back thousands of years. Each has developed its own language, its own dress, and its own distinct cuisine. In the country as a whole, there are over sixteen hundred different languages and dialects, a fact that makes communication difficult among people of the same nation. The people even look different, depending on their region: the stocky, dark-skinned South Indian wrapped in white cloth seems a world apart from the tall, fair-skinned, light-eyed North Indians of Aryan origin.

And then, within each community are the differences of caste and of class. Hinduism—India's majority religion—lays down four main castes, which form a strictly hierarchical basis for Indian society. At the top of the ladder are the Brahmins, or the priests and religious men. Then come the Kshatriyas, or warriors; then the traders; and last of all, the menial workers. Membership in a caste is hereditary, and, over the years, the four original castes have subdivided into thousands of smaller subcastes, based upon area and occupation.

In the twentieth century, the lines of caste have blurred with those of class. The most apparent differences in India today are between the rich and the poor. Upward mobility—although easier now than it was fifty years ago—is still difficult, and it seems as though the poor will always remain poor. And so, while landless laborers and menial workers have barely enough to feed and clothe their families, the elite lifestyle is comparable to any the world over.

Finally, among the people of India there are the differences to be found in a feudal society that was pushed too fast into the twentieth century. Villages without roads or electricity remain locked in their own timeless world, barely aware of another life outside their doorstep; to many of the villagers, Indira Gandhi was probably the queen of India. While in the cities, the east and west, the past and the future exist on the same plane, creating situations that are incongruous and often chaotic.

It is often said that India is an example of unity amidst diversity. The diversity is only too apparent. The unity, however, remains still to be tested by time. Indeed, there are few unifying factors to hold together the seventh largest nation in the world. The comparative isolation of the subcontinent has given its people a certain similarity or homogeneity, a few typical characteristics that westerners identify as the 'Indian character,' but they are hardly strong enough to forge a strong national identity.

Hinduism, the faith of 78.8 percent of India's population, is the single most unifying factor in India. It provides a thread of cultural unity, based on a common religious literature and folklore, and a deep-rooted tradition of continuity. At Hindu weddings, for example, priests dressed in white muslin chant the same hymns they did thirty-five hundred years ago. Nevertheless, Hinduism is not as strong a uniting force as the world's younger religions, Islam and Christianity. Unlike these religions, Hinduism has no prescribed doctrine or scripture, and no single deity. Hinduism is more a philosophy, a way of life that does not profess to be the only path to salvation. Its scriptures are a vast, amorphous body of work written over centuries; within its folds, Hinduism offers different ways of leading a good life, and many paths to salvation.

Because of its diversity, India has rarely been ruled as one country. In the course of nearly three thousand years of recorded history, only a handful of rulers have succeeded in bringing a major portion of the country under their sway, and not a single one of them has succeeded in penetrating to the southern tip of the peninsula. It was only the British, with the help of improved communications, who were able to rule the country as one for almost two hundred years. But even the British left two-fifths of the country to be ruled by the Indians themselves, and the unity they imposed was merely administrative, not cultural or social.

Before the British arrived in India, the country had been controlled for centuries by a succession of Muslim rulers. The most significant Muslim dynasty in India was the Mughals. The word Mughal is an Indianization of the word Mongol, but applies only to this particular dynasty. The Mughals, who came from Samarkand in central Asia, ruled India from the sixteenth century to the nineteenth. Northern India flourished under the enlightened rule of these able monarchs. One of the Mughal kings, Shah Jahan, built the beautiful Taj Mahal, the marble monument that immortalized his love for his wife, Mumtaz Mahal. The southern part of India had followed its own course; it was divided into small kingdoms—both Hindu and Muslim.

In keeping with the Muslim tradition, the rulers encouraged conversion to Islam. Although Hinduism survived the onslaught, Islam, too, became a part of India; today, Muslims are found in every corner of the country, and in every social class. Hindi, India's official national language, is a legacy of Muslim rule, and Muslim influence pervades Indian society, especially in the arts and architecture. Tensions between

Hindus and Muslims, however, have always remained, and have always flared up at the slightest provocation, throughout the latter part of Indian history. These inherent tensions were further inflamed by the British, with their policy of "divide and rule."

Europeans came to India initially to trade in spices. The Portuguese came to India in 1498, even before the Mughals, and the French, Dutch, and British followed.

The British came to India as "The East India Company," a private commercial enterprise that received a charter from Queen Elizabeth I to trade with the "Indies"—which included India, China, and Indonesia. Throughout the seventeenth century, the company operated on a small scale from ports granted to them by the Mughals. The ports grew into India's principal cities of Madras, Bombay, and Calcutta. In the power vacuum that followed the disintegration of the Mughal Empire, the British moved in and established their supremacy over India. The conquest of India was achieved by the East India Company with the help of ships from the Royal Navy, and Indian regiments trained by the British. Then, in 1858, Queen Victoria issued a proclamation that finally put the Indian empire into the hands of the British Government itself.

British rule in India was based on the premise of the supremacy of the light-skinned "master race." This fact was rubbed into the Indians by the "Europeans only" signs that came up outside clubs, outside first-class railway carriages, and even on park benches.

Foreigners had conquered and ruled India since the dawn of Indian history, but all of them were gradually absorbed into the Indian culture, so that they no longer remained foreign to the country. The British in India, however, remained foreigners until they left in 1947, after a long freedom struggle by the Indians.

Besides the fact that British rule brought political unification to India for the first time in its long history, the most apparent legacy of the British Raj, the period of British rule, is the English language. Although Hindi is the national language, most official correspondence is conducted in English, and, in the cities, signs, advertisements, and television programs are mostly in English. The British also brought the concept of mass education to India. Earlier, formal education had been a prerogative of the Indian upper classes. And, although the literacy rate was barely 17 percent when the British left India, they had set up schools and colleges and implanted the concept of mass education in the Indian consciousness.

The drawbacks of British rule in India were those of all colonial rule the world over—India was ruled for the economic benefit of Britain. India had a rich tradition of cottage industry; weaving and pottery were highly developed arts, passed down from father to son. But these crafts suffered when the Indian market was flooded with cheap consumer goods made in England. Cotton grown in India, for example, was sent to England, where it was spun and woven into cloth in the mills of Manchester. The finished cloth was then re-exported to India. Thus, India did not develop an industrial economy of its own, and in the twentieth century remained an agrarian economy with no industrial base.

When the British left India, it was a feudal, caste-based society whose mainstay was agriculture. Its food production, however, was not enough to feed its fast-growing population, and there were no means to support the legion of landless laborers, who had no option but to live in grinding poverty.

It was under these circumstances that an independent India attempted the great democratic experiment. In a largely illiterate society, with a majority of its people only dimly aware of its rulers, India opted for universal franchise—it granted a vote to every adult citizen. India's democratic government is based on the British parliamentary system. The Indian Parliament is divided into two houses, the *Rajya Sabha* (House of States) and the *Lok Sabha* (House of Commons). The governing body is the *Lok Sabha*, whose members are elected directly by the people.

India has many political parties, and it is the party with a majority of seats in the *Lok Sabha* that forms the government. The leader of the ruling party becomes prime minister. India does have a president, who is officially the head of the country, but he is a figurehead, much like the British monarch; the actual power is vested in the office of the prime minister. As in Britain, the people do not vote directly for their prime minister, but for the party candidate representing their constituency. Each party, however, usually names its leader before the elections, so that the people know who they are actually voting in as prime minister. India also borrowed from the United States the concept of federalism, in which individual states have certain powers. India has twenty-two states, each with its own legislature, and in theory, power is shared by the central government and the governments of the individual states.

India's democracy sets it apart from most Third World countries, which have remained dictatorships. For example, India allows its people freedom of speech, religion, and assembly. India is also set apart from other Third World countries in the level of economic development it has achieved. On attaining independence, the nation tried to modernize. Equating technological progress with economic well-being, the government set a priority on developing heavy industry. Now, thirty-seven years after independence, the country grows enough food to feed its people, ranks among the world's top fifteen in industrial output, and has the ability to train its own scientists and technicians.

However, problems remain for this young democracy. The most pressing problem in India today is its population. Western medicine has improved health care, so that the death rate has fallen dramatically. The birth rate, however, has not, and India today has the second largest population in the world. It often seems that all planning and progress are drowned in the ever increasing sea of humanity.

Almost 40 percent of India's population lives in absolute poverty, and the life expectancy of the individual is far lower than in developed countries like the United States. In fact, India today faces all the problems that characterize a developing nation: its villages remain locked in poverty, while industrialized cities attract throngs of fortune seekers, so that they seem to be bursting at the seams. The gap between the rich and the poor seems impossible to bridge, and an inefficient, corrupt bureaucracy threatens to strangle progress in any direction.

Added to that are the problems peculiar to India's complex, multilayered society: tensions between castes and communities seem to simmer always under the surface, ready to explode into violence at the slightest provocation. India requires a strong leader to hold this chaotic, complex country together. In a still largely feudal society, the prime minister must also be charismatic, to be able to sway the popular imagination, rather than appeal to the intellect. Indira Gandhi gave India this kind of leadership for more than sixteen years.

Being prime minister of India has often been compared to riding a tiger—once you get on, there is no way of getting off, and no way of knowing which way you will go. For Indira Gandhi, this analogy was most appropriate.

A LONELY CHILDHOOD

3

On meeting Indira Gandhi, people were often struck by her reserve, and the sad, lonely look in her large black eyes. Once, when a visiting journalist asked her to describe Indira Gandhi the woman, she replied after a pause, "In spite of living in the public glare, she has remained a very private person. Her life has been hard. This has made her self-reliant, but has not hardened her."

Indira Priyadarshini—the second name means "dear to behold"—was born November 19, 1917, the only child of Jawaharlal Nehru and his wife Kamala in the city of Allahabad in Northern India. In the Indian tradition, theirs was a joint family, headed by Indira's grandfather, Motilal Nehru, a man with a magnetic personality and an enormous zest for life. His loud, infectious laughter, Indira remembered, "shook the whole house." Allahabad had a high court, and Motilal, a self-made man, was one of the most successful barristers in his time. With success came wealth, and the Nehru family lived in a sprawling whitewashed villa, surrounded by lawns, tennis courts, and a swimming pool, and attended by a legion of servants. Being the only child in this huge household, Indira was petted and pampered and was the center of her grandfather's attention. Then, when she was barely three, the Indian freedom movement entered the Nehru house, changing Indira's life and the course of Indian history.

Jawaharlal Nehru had come into contact with Mohandas Karamchand Gandhi, who became the venerated leader of India's freedom struggle, and his imagination had been captured by Gandhi's advocation of nonviolent resistance to British rule. Motilal, however, thought the idea of courting arrest ridiculous, and the Nehru household rang with heated exchanges between father and son. Things might have continued in this way indefinitely had it not been for the Jallianwalla Bag massacre.

On April 13, 1919, at a peaceful public meeting, British troops fired on an unarmed crowd of twenty thousand men, women, and children, killing 379 and wounding over 1,200 before they ran out of ammunition. Motilal and many others like him, who, until then, had believed in the ultimate benevolence of British rule in India, found their illusions shattered overnight.

Motilal was drawn toward Gandhi, and the Nehru family committed itself to Gandhi's brand of nonviolent noncooperation. The family also supported Gandhi's policy of promoting indigenous cottage industries by boycotting all foreign goods. The change this action brought to the Nehru house-

From the time Indira was a young child, family life centered on the movement to free India from British colonial rule. She is shown here in 1935 with Mohandas Gandhi, the leader of the freedom movement.

hold was dramatic. Motilal, who never did anything half-heartedly, folded up his legal practice, abandoned his Saville Row suits for homespun (*khadi*) clothes, sold his horses and carriages, dismissed most of his servants, and directed his energies toward the struggle for independence.

The drama of the moment was not lost on the young Indira, whose first vivid memory was of the day her family burned all its foreign possessions. "I can still feel the excitement of the day and see the large terrace covered with piles of clothes—what rich materials, what lovely colors! What fun for a toddler to jump in, play hide-and-seek in the heaps of velvets, satins, and chiffons!" says Indira in her autobiography.

At that time, Motilal was the president of the Indian National Congress. Founded in 1885, it served as a sort of opposition party to British rule in India, and had begun demanding independence from British rule. After the Jallianwalla Bag episode, the Congress officially adopted Gandhi's policy of nonviolent agitation.

Motilal's involvement with the Congress made his home the hub of the freedom movement. It became a place where earnest, *khadi*-clad men came and went at all hours of the day and night; it became a place that rang with drafts, declarations, and debates. Indira absorbed the tension and excitement of those days and became a quiet, serious child, fired by a sense of mission she did not quite comprehend. She remembered climbing onto the dining table and regaling the servants with thunderous speeches compiled of overheard slogans and phrases. "I haven't the remotest idea what I said to them," she recalled.

Even Indira's games were political ones. Her dolls were divided into freedom fighters, who formed picket lines, and British soldiers, who clubbed them on the head and dragged them off to jail. Her aunt remembers discovering Indira on the veranda, eyes burning, arms dramatically outstretched, playing Joan of Arc leading her people to freedom. By the time she was twelve, Indira was making a real effort to be involved in the struggle. She formed the Vanar Sena, or Monkey Brigade, a group of children who ran errands and acted as couriers for their elders, a role usually played by women in times of war.

Indira discovered soon, however, that the family's commitment to the freedom movement meant more than just fun and games. For the Nehrus, who were permanently in the forefront of the movement, the twenty-five long years of civil disobedience and jail sentences meant a suspension of family life. From the age of four, Indira was periodically deprived of the companionship of those she loved most, and denied a normal childhood. Almost as wearing as the long separations was the suspense that clouded their brief reunions. Any knock on the door could mean that the police had come again to remove one of her family to jail. Being an only child made her situation far worse. Indira was often left alone in the large house, or shunted off to live with distant relatives.

In spite of the uncertain nature of her family's life, Indira was not, in the normal sense, neglected or deprived. Her parents were constantly concerned for her welfare, and her father wrote to her regularly. In fact, as a present for her thirteenth birthday, he undertook to give her a correspondence course in world history. These letters, though written without reference books from a prison cell, are a perceptive interpretation of world events. (Called "Glimpses of World History," the letters were later published, but at the time he wrote them, Nehru confessed it was for his own pleasure. "They bring you near me," he said, "and I feel I have to talk.")

Often, his letters showed an understanding of his child's loneliness. On New Year's Day, 1931, he wrote, "Often enough, I think of you, but today you have hardly been absent from my mind. Today is New Year's Day . . . but you must be rather lonely. Once a fortnight you may see

Mummie [who was also in jail], and once a fortnight you may see me, and you will carry our messages to each other."

Her mother, Kamala, was with Indira more often than her father, and, according to Indira, formed the strongest influence of her life. Mostly ignored by her husband and scorned by his mother and sisters because of her lack of sophistication and her ignorance of Western ways, Indira's mother was an intense, quiet woman who was often sick. Kamala was devoted to Indira, and Indira responded by identifying completely with her mother. For Indira, her mother's suffering was an early introduction to unhappiness, and often she responded by withdrawing into herself so as not to appear vulnerable. "I saw her being hurt," she said later, "and I was determined not to be hurt."

Indira's schooling, too, was not free of the shadow of her traumatic home life. By the time she was thirteen she had changed school six times—including a two-year stretch in Switzerland with her sick mother. As a result, Indira showed little interest in her studies, and formed no lasting friendships among her schoolmates. Dressed in rough, sackcloth-like homespun, she always felt different from other children, and their conventional games held little interest for her. She preferred to play alone.

Influenced by the insecurities of her childhood, Indira grew up into a thin, solemn-eyed girl who seldom laughed. She was painfully shy and withdrawn, and usually appeared tense and fidgety. These traits remained with her until the end. Although she later lost her awkward ways, she was usually reserved and distant in small gatherings, and except with her family and a few close friends, she was rarely relaxed.

Indira's completion of school, just after her sixteenth birthday, was greeted by a telegram from her father informing her that he was once again going to jail, and, even more disturbing, that her mother, who was suspected of having tuberculosis, had taken a turn for the worse. After spending some time nursing her, the young Indira was sent to Shantiniketan (meaning "abode of peace"), an unconventional, informal university in Bengal founded by Rabindranath Tagore, a Nobel prize–winning poet and philosopher.

Her stay at the university, which she considered among the most peaceful and relaxed times in her life, lasted only a year. In May 1935, with her father still in jail, seventeen-year-old Indira was once again sent off to Switzerland with her sick mother. There was no cure for TB then, but Nehru sent his wife to Europe in hopes that the clean mountain air would help her to recover from the dreaded disease. Indira entered her mother in a sanitarium, and stayed at a pension nearby. Instead of improving, Kamala's health deteriorated rapidly. A friend who met Indira during these months informed her father that she was "in a piteous state of mind, having been told that her mother was dying." In September, Nehru was released from jail on compassionate grounds and joined his family in Switzerland. Although Kamala's health showed some improvement after Nehru's arrival, she died a few months later, on February 28, 1936. Indira had faced death before. Her grandfather had died when she was fourteen, but he had led a full life. Kamala was only thirty-six, and Indira was devastated when she died.

While Nehru was in Switzerland, he received word that he had been elected president of the Congress party by proxy. He had become an important leader of the Indian freedom movement, and toward the end of his stay in Switzerland, he had been "straining at the leash," eager to return to India. Now, after a short time with his grief-stricken daughter, he left for home, instructing Indira to continue her studies in England. This almost ruthless action was typical of Nehru. Although his letters to Indira were regular and full of concern, there is no question that Nehru neglected his wife and child. Always, in those days, politics came first.

In her long years of loneliness, Indira had learned to be self-reliant, but after her mother's death, she seemed to lose her moorings. For the next five years, she shunted restlessly back and forth between England, India, and Switzerland. During this time she studied sporadically.

When she was in England, Indira was often seen with another young foreign student, Feroze Gandhi. Feroze had been a frequent visitor to the Nehru household, although it had been Indira's mother Kamala who he usually came to see. A few years earlier, he had been standing nearby when Kamala collapsed during an anti-British demonstration outside his college in Allahabad. He had carried her home, and become very fond of her. Feroze was a common sight in the Nehru household, and he often nursed Kamala through her long, lonely bouts of sickness. Although he did not pay special attention to Indira, who was five years his junior, they probably got to know each other quite well. Feroze was studying at the London School of Economics while Kamala was ill in Switzerland, and he came to see her often. In England, after her mother's death, Indira was alone in a foreign country for the first time in her life and depressed. Not surprisingly, she found herself drawn towards Feroze.

In February 1941, with London ravaged by war and the Indian freedom movement reaching an apparent confrontation with the British, the young couple cut short their studies, decided to get married, and sailed for home. "Up to the age of eighteen or nineteen, I was determined that I would never marry," Indira Gandhi told an interviewer, "because I felt I should devote every minute of my time to the political struggle, and marriage would come in the way. But then, when I decided to get married, I just didn't think out things anymore. I just got married."

Indira with her
father in 1938

Indira's family, however, did not welcome the news that she intended to marry Feroze. Jawaharlal Nehru, in fact, vehemently opposed the match, in spite of the fact that Indira and Feroze had been friends for many years. He was not considered a suitable mate for Indira.

Feroze Gandhi had the same surname as Mohandas Gandhi, the leader of India's freedom struggle, but he came from quite a different social and religious background. Unlike Mohandas, who was a Hindu, Feroze was a Parsi, a member of one of the smallest and most cohesive religious sects in India. The Parsis, who fled from Persia over a thousand years ago to escape Muslim persecution, have lived in harmony in India with other religious sects. They are a highly cultured, literate community, jealous of their cultural identity.

The Nehrus, on the other hand, were Hindus of the highest caste. They were Brahmins from the mountain state of Kashmir, and their community of Kashmiri Pandits remains, even today, an exclusive one. Nehru's objections to his daughter's marriage, however, were based on class considerations rather than on religion. The Nehrus were aristocrats, with a fierce clannish pride that sometimes struck outsiders as arrogance. Feroze, on the other hand, was aggressively proud of his lower middle-class background, and made no secret of his impatience with the Nehru exclusiveness. Besides, Feroze had no money and no job, and Nehru was not sure that he would be able to maintain Indira in the style to which she was accustomed.

The position of the Nehru family in Indian politics ensured that the controversy over Indira's choice of a husband would move into the public arena. Mohandas Gandhi's nonviolent movement was now widespread in India, and Gandhi himself was widely revered and known as Mahatma or "great soul." Jawaharlal Nehru, too, had risen to become a charismatic leader, and Gandhi had publicly chosen him as his "heir." Nehru was popular with people throughout the country; his daughter's marriage, therefore, aroused great interest.

Traditionally, matches in India are arranged by parents, and the spouse usually belongs to the same community and social background. Even though marriages of choice, or "love" marriages, are becoming more common, interreligious marriages still raise eyebrows. Orthodox Hindus were so outraged that Indira had chosen to marry a Parsi that Jawaharlal, . and even Gandhi, were forced to come to Indira's defense publicly. In an editorial in his weekly newspaper, *The Harijan*, Mahatma Gandhi wrote, "I have received several angry and abusive letters, and some professing to reason about Indira's engagement to Feroze Gandhi. Not a single correspondent has anything against Feroze Gandhi as a man. His only crime, in their estimation, is that he happens to be a Parsi."

To Indira, it indicated just how much the Nehrus lived in the public eye. "It seems that the whole world was against the marriage," she lamented later. This was the first time the previously irresolute and pliable young girl had asserted herself so vigorously, and the first time she had opposed her strong-willed father. This apparent contradiction in her character, however, turned out to be a consistent behavior pattern with her. Even as prime minister, she would drift submissively for long periods; then, when she had made up her mind, she would act with a confidence and decisiveness that never failed to amaze those who thought they knew her. Now, although her family was surprised at this stubborn streak, once they realized that Indira was serious, they agreed to the match. The couple was married in the Nehru home on March 26, 1942. Indira looked radiant in a shell-pink *khadi* sari her father had spun for her while serving a term in prison.

A few months after her wedding, Indira, herself, was jailed, an event she referred to later as the most dramatic incident in her life. Courting arrest was a Congress policy, a way of protesting to the British Raj, and Indira's nine months in jail marked for her a political coming of age. Some leaders used their time in prison for writing and for reflecting on the course of political events. Indira's father, for example, was an introspective man. For Nehru, whose various prison terms totalled nine years, those years in jail were the most fertile in his intellectual development. It was in jail that he developed his political ideas, and wrote his best books. For Indira, however, things were different. She was a doer, not a thinker, and isolation from the world imposed a great strain on her. "(It) . . . was like coming out of a dark passage . . . just to touch and listen was a disturbing experience . . ." she wrote when released from jail.

Feroze, who had been in jail also, was released a while later, and the couple settled down to married life. They took a small house in the city of Lucknow, where Feroze became the managing director of *The National Herald*, a newspaper that had been founded by his father-in-law. Two sons, Rajiv and Sanjay, were born in quick succession, and it seemed that Indira was ready to settle down in her role as wife and mother.

Following the end of World War II, the British Government was convinced, at last, that it could no longer rule India. In September 1946, Jawaharlal Nehru became the head of an "interim" government and on August 15, 1947, the first prime minister of independent India. The Indian people had long dreamed of this moment, and when it came, Indira remembers being too numb to feel anything.

Now, with freedom won, came the most significant decision in Indira's life. Should she give up politics and concentrate on being a wife and mother, or should she follow her father into the arena of Indian politics? It was a decision that Indira, by all indications, did not consciously make. Her father, living alone in his large official mansion, increasingly needed someone to host his formal dinners for world dignitaries. Indira found herself shuttling back and forth between Lucknow and New Delhi to act as hostess for Nehru.

Indira's husband, however, did not always appreciate her absence. And there were other causes of conflict. The two were essentially different. Indira, with her patrician refinement and reserve, found it difficult to put up with Feroze's brash, hearty manner, and his often bawdy sense of humor. The couple began to drift apart as Indira spent more time with her father in New Delhi. Later, with her two sons, she moved into her father's residence. Although her husband, too, tried to live there for a time, the arrangement did not work well, and Feroze, who had been elected a member of Parliament, moved into his own little house in the capital. This, in effect, was the end of Indira's marriage. Although the two were never officially divorced, they went their separate ways. Feroze, in fact, was often openly critical of Nehru. By the time he died of a heart attack in 1960, Feroze Gandhi had built himself a reputation as a "champion of the underdog."

Gradually Indira became a sort of "first lady." She accompanied Nehru everywhere. She walked a few steps behind her illustrious father, always quiet, always ready to be of use, always immaculately dressed. She followed him on long, dusty roads in the searing heat. At mass meetings she sat quietly behind him, and sometimes, when Nehru couldn't attend, she spoke for him. She hosted his functions, and she smiled gracefully at diplomatic parties. With her father she traveled to Moscow, to Peking, and three times to Washington. But although Nehru trusted Indira and often confided in her, she held no political status. She knew everyone, but no one took her very seriously.

It is often said that Indira chose to be with her father because she wished to be near the seat of power. It seems clear, however, that although she probably became politically ambitious in the final years of Nehru's life, initially she just

Acting as Nehru's unofficial "First Lady" and living in the state residence with her two sons, Indira's marriage quietly ended, though she and Feroze never actually divorced. Nehru, Indira and her sons, Sanjay and Rajiv (at right), were photographed with President and Mrs. Sukarno of Indonesia and their son and daughter in 1950.

drifted into her role, drawn by her father's loneliness and need, and pushed by her own unhappiness with her marriage. She did not, in fact, enjoy the job, despite its surface glamour. She confessed that she did not like housekeeping, and she was painfully shy at social functions. She was, at the time, rather confused about her future. "What a life I have made for myself," she wrote to a friend in 1955. "Often, I seem to be standing outside myself, watching and wondering if it's all worth the trouble."

HER FATHER'S SHADOW

4

While in England, and still a student dabbling with leftist ideas, Indira went to the economist Harold Laski for advice on her future. "If you want to amount to something," he said, "you had better start your own life right now. If you tag along with your father, you won't be able to do anything else."

He couldn't have been more wrong. In retrospect, it seems that it was precisely by "tagging along" with her father that Indira became one of the world's most powerful women. But at the time, she didn't see it that way. She went along with her father, she wrote to her friend, New York–based writer and photographer Dorothy Norman, because "there doesn't seem to be any choice, in the sense that I felt my father's loneliness so intensely, and I felt also that whatever I amounted to, or whatever satisfaction I got from my own work, would not, from a wide perspective, be so useful as my 'tagging along'. . . ."

"Life does not run according to our desires or expectations," Indira Gandhi wrote, with some regret, "and when India became free, I was catapulted into a new life and involved in new responsibilities which have grown considerably over the years. At first, it was only a question of setting up a home for my father in New Delhi and coping with the social obligations of the Prime Minister's House. But, gradually, circumstances, and my own interest in the path which my country was trying to follow, drew me deeper into public affairs." Soon she became a part of the complex process of lobbying and decision-making that characterize Indian politics.

The fifties were India's years of hope. The nonviolent struggle that had won India its independence from British rule had also won it the admiration of the world. And, as Mahatma Gandhi had predicted, the movement had drawn to it dedicated, visionary leaders like Jawaharlal Nehru, Sardar Vallabhai Patel, and Rajendra Prasad, who now held positions of power in free India.

With his patrician good looks, his intense air, and his polished blend of East and West, Nehru was an ideal—and idealistic—leader for the new India. As prime minister, he took upon himself the mammoth task of modernizing the vast, still-feudal nation, choosing the path of democratic socialism. Abroad, he pursued a policy of fierce anticolonialism, and, in 1960, became the founder of the nonaligned movement, organizing a group of nations that professed to be aligned to neither the Soviet Union nor the United States. Nehru was cosmopolitan, commanding, and, above all, charismatic. In the course of the freedom struggle, he had emerged as a national figure; now, as the country's first democratically appointed leader, he commanded the adulation of the people and the respect of his colleagues.

In his shadow, Indira had been a part of the freedom struggle. Now, at his side, she learned the intricate workings of post-independence party politics and the subtle rules of the international power play. Although she always kept a low public profile, she developed a shrewd political insight and a sound sense of timing, qualities that were to remain her biggest assets throughout her career. In these years of apprenticeship, she forged a tough, pragmatic style, so that gradually, the introspective, often gullible, Nehru began to depend more and more upon her political advice.

Also, in this period, Indira discovered that she had the ability to sway crowds. Years before, her first public speech, at a meeting of the "India League" in England, had been a disaster. "She doesn't speak, she squeaks," someone in the audience had roared. The mortified Indira had vowed never to speak in public again. But now, helping her father to canvass for the first general election in 1951, this shy young woman, who was always awkward at social gatherings, was delighted to discover that she could communicate with crowds. She recalled later the excitement she felt in one of her earlier talks in a remote village in the northwestern state of Punjab.

It was a cold and misty January morning with a sharp breeze and at 6 A.M. still quite dark. Not a soul was in sight. All doors and windows seemed to be tightly secured. However, there was a takhat *[platform] and a microphone and some* durries *[carpets], wet with heavy dew. Hansrajji [a senior Congressman at the time] felt that we had done our duty by coming and we could now drive on to the regular program with a clear conscience. However, much to his embarrassment, I insisted on giving a speech whether there was anybody to listen or not. Almost with my first word, windows started banging open and tousled heads appeared. Immediately afterwards the entire village poured out from the warmth of their houses, wrapped in blankets and* razais *[quilts], some with* dattun *sticks [a sort of toothbrush], and some with tumblers of steaming tea. . . ."*

When she first began speaking, Indira filled in for her father, and her audiences were small. Nehru was an accomplished orator, and his speeches were flowery and long. Indira, however, had a direct and down-to-earth manner, and her mass appeal increased. Although she never ran for office while Nehru lived, she became, gradually, a public figure with a national following.

Hindu ideology has always had a dual role for its women. On one hand she is the saint Savitri, the docile, self-sacrificing wife and mother. On the other, she is the fierce goddess Durga, who rides a tiger and drinks the blood of her enemies. In practice, however, the women were usually in the home, until Gandhi called upon them to join the freedom struggle. He preached equality of the sexes, and, at his insistence, women came out of their homes. They joined the picket lines, they were clubbed by policemen, they went to jail, and, along with the men, they received their share of the limelight. When India became independent, it seemed quite natural for them to remain active politically, and women held positions of power that seemed inconsistent in an inherently traditional society. In the India of the 60s, there was, in fact, less resistance to women in power than in a nontraditional country like the United States. Nevertheless, being Nehru's daughter freed Indira from any lingering limitations imposed by her sex. At the same time, in spite of her growing influence over her father, she was not seen as a threat to him or to other male politicians. Had it been a son at his side, there would have been accusations of nepotism, or favoritism to family members, as there were later, when Mrs. Gandhi's son Sanjay became powerful.

Under the circumstances, Indira achieved, as one of her biographers notes, the apparently impossible: she remained inconspicuously, but permanently, in the public eye, and was able, without attracting hostility, to build a national image, and a cohesive power base for herself. Whether or not Nehru deliberately groomed her to be his heir is a question that has been hotly debated, but never conclusively answered. It was clear that he was very proud of her, and would probably have liked to see her in a position of power. Even his critics admit, however, that Nehru was too much of a democrat to actually promote a dynastic succession.

In February 1955, when she was almost forty, Indira Gandhi made her official debut into Indian politics. She became a member of the twenty-one member Working Committee of the Congress party, an administrative post that she fulfilled conscientiously, although colleagues remember her as being rather shy and saying very little at party meetings. She had always been active in organizing charities and promoting social welfare, and this she continued to do, with the added backing of her party position.

In 1959, Indira Gandhi was made the president of the Indian National Congress, a post that both her father and her grandfather had held before her. This was her first important position. Although she claimed that Nehru disapproved of her accepting the post, a report that he himself corroborated, it is generally acknowledged that Nehru pulled strings from behind the scenes—just as his father had done for him thirty years earlier—to get his daughter this prestigious position.

The Congress party of the 1950s, however, was a democratic one, and Nehru, even at the height of his power, could not have foisted his daughter on the party had its members been opposed to the idea. Clearly, Indira had managed to build a reputation for herself, apart from the authority that came from being her father's daughter.

When Indira took up her duties as head of the party, the Congress bosses were expecting to deal with a mild, ineffectual president. She surprised everyone, however, with her tough, pragmatic handling of her first important political position. She was energetic and practical. At her first press conference she said, "The nation is in a hurry, and we can't

afford to lose time. My complaint against the Congress is that it isn't going as fast as the people are advancing. And that can be fatal for a political organization."

It was twelve years after independence, and the Congress party, made up of aging leaders of the freedom struggle, was becoming increasingly bureaucratic and ponderous. Indira, who brought a young, leftist image to her office, tried to change the party's structure and approach by encouraging younger, radical members to move into positions of power. She also sought to increase the participation of women in the party. During her first three months, Indira traveled throughout the country, attracting large crowds of women and students with speeches that reflected her socialist convictions.

She was not, however, able to make much of an impact on the party organization. The most important event during her presidency, in fact, was her role in overthrowing the government of the state of Kerala.

In 1957, the southern state of Kerala, which had the highest literacy rate in India, had elected a Communist government. It was the first non-Congress government of independent India, and the first Communist government in the world to come into power through parliamentary elections. Its radical policies, however, had alienated the conservative, caste-based opposition parties. By 1959, the opposition was planning to band together to form a united front, aimed at overthrowing the Communist party. The Congress party in Kerala was eager to join the front, although the other parties

Indira accompanied Nehru to Washington to meet with President Eisenhower in 1956. During the years at her father's side, Indira was highly visible but politically insignificant.

had traditionally been its enemies. Nehru was not very happy about Congress involvement in the front. In April 1959, he sent Indira to survey the situation and report back to him.

Since Indira had openly professed her leftist ideas, the Communist government expected her to be sympathetic to their cause. She surprised everyone, however, when, even against the wishes of her father, she advised the Congress party to join the anti-Communist front, and to launch a "peaceful, nonviolent, and constitutional" movement against the government in power. When the situation turned violent, the central Congress leadership demanded that the national government take responsibility for governing the state, claiming that the Communist government was unable to control the situation. Mrs. Gandhi's speeches grew more militantly anti-Communist. She even went so far as to tell the press, ". . . if the constitution has no remedy for the people of Kerala, the constitution should be amended," a statement that she was forced to withdraw later, under fire.

Finally, on July 31, the president of India dismissed the government of Kerala and brought the province under temporary central rule. Mrs. Gandhi played an important role in the negotiations that led to a Congress alliance with the other opposition parties to form a "united front." On December 8, an election was held to choose a new state government for Kerala. Led by the Congress party, the opposition "united front" won. The Congress itself, however, drew only 34 percent of the votes, while the Communist party got 44 percent.

With her success in bringing Kerala back into the fold, Mrs. Gandhi indicated for the first time that she was a master at the art of political maneuvering. Her actions also showed Mrs. Gandhi's perception of politics. In spite of having grown up in the shadow of her idealistic father, she saw politics essentially as power play. She abandoned her leftist ideology as soon as it proved inconvenient, and she was prepared to be ruthless to achieve her ends. The "Kerala approach"—in which the Congress party, in fact, helped incite the violence that it claimed as an excuse to take over an opposition-led state government—was later to become Mrs. Gandhi's formula for dealing with opposition governments. At the time, however, the move failed to cause much of a furor in Parliament. It blew over soon, and Mrs. Gandhi emerged with her reputation intact.

The Congress party president usually holds the post for two years, but Mrs. Gandhi stepped down after one year, announcing that she intended to devote all her time to her father. "I have gained tremendously in self confidence," she wrote to a friend, just before resigning, "but I do not wish to continue for many reasons. The routine part of the work takes too much time and is too confining. I have felt like a bird in a too-small cage. Also, I feel that I have now established myself and will be able to do quite a lot even from outside . . ."

Two years later, in 1962, a border skirmish with China brought a drastic change in India's self-image, as well as a change in Nehru himself. The brief war began as a minor border dispute over some barren land deep in the snow-covered Himalayas. Nehru adopted a dogmatic stance that spurned negotiations. Suspicions escalated on both sides until, on October 20, China attacked. India was caught completely unprepared for its first war; ten days later, China withdrew, leaving Indian defenses in shambles.

One of the most startling outcomes of the war was its effect on Nehru. Past seventy, and having served in office for more than a decade, Nehru was becoming increasingly disillusioned and crotchety. He had had great hopes and plans for India, and now, toward the end of his life, he felt that few had been realized. The Indochina war, however, demoralized him completely. His policies were now criticized openly in India and abroad, and Nehru did not have the spirit to defend them. He began to leave things to his daughter, who still kept a low profile. Outsiders, who often saw Nehru snap at Indira, still thought of her as Nehru's shadow, but those who had access to the "inner circle" realized that, in the last two years of Nehru's life, Indira was the "power behind the throne." In fact, in his book *After Nehru, Who?*, published in 1963, American journalist Welles Hangen included Indira Gandhi among the eight people most likely to succeed Nehru. Hangen did not, however, think that Indira—whose imperious, regal ways reminded him of a Hapsburg Empress—would be India's next prime minister:

> *It is her misfortune that she will lose her most precious key to power (her father's backing) the moment she needs it most, when her father's passing has left an empty room at the top. Without the key, I doubt that Indira Gandhi can open the door to that room.*

When Nehru died of a stroke on May 28, 1964, Indira was never seriously considered as India's next prime minister. According to the Indian constitution, the prime minister is to be elected by the majority party. In the last years of Nehru's rule, state chief ministers, as well as party bosses, were becoming increasingly powerful within the Congress party, and jockeying for the position of prime minister had already begun.

In fact, by 1963 Lal Bahadur Shastri and Morarji Desai had emerged as the leading contenders. Finally, Shastri, a small, unassuming man who had started his career as a sort of retainer to the Nehrus, was chosen prime minister. He asked Indira Gandhi to join his cabinet as minister of information and broadcasting, overseeing the state-owned radio stations. It was a relatively unimportant post, and it was reported that Indira would have preferred to be foreign minister. Nevertheless, she accepted the position.

In 1964 Indira was sworn in as Information Minister,
the relatively unimportant post offered to her
by her father's successor, Prime Minister Shastri.

Nehru's death had been a great blow to his only daughter. For the first time in her life she was alone, left to fend for herself and her two sons. For the next few months, she seemed disoriented, tended to burst into tears often, and told people she wanted "to retire to the mountains."

She moved from the large, official Teen Murti house into the modest, four-bedroom residence given to her as cabinet minister. There she lived alone, since both her sons were studying in England. Indira's performance as minister of information and broadcasting was unspectacular. In public meetings and at private interviews, however, she hinted at her dissatisfaction with the Shastri government in a manner that assured that she was often in the public eye. Then came the first war with Pakistan in 1965, and Mrs. Gandhi's exploits won her the title of the "only man in a cabinet of old women."

Always, ever since she had led protest marches during the freedom struggle, Mrs. Gandhi had demonstrated that she was fearless. "I have been accused of many things," she said once, "but never of lack of courage." Now, during the war, she visited dangerous border areas—often against the advice of air force officials—and gave rallying speeches that helped to preserve the morale of the armed forces, and of the people.

Although the war was short, and did not end in a decisive victory for either side, the Indian army made important gains and Indian morale revived after its collapse in 1962. As a result, Prime Minister Shastri, who had often been a butt of humor until then, became something of a hero overnight. But his time in the limelight was brief, for he died suddenly of a heart attack in January 1966.

People who had predicted chaos and an end to democracy in India after Nehru's death were even more convinced of it now, when Shastri died. Nehru's illness had been long and death had been foreseen for months, whereas Shastri's end was sudden, and the young democracy had no time to prepare a successor. To fill the void, the ruling Congress party promptly chose Indira Gandhi as its leader and prime minister. The transition of power was a smooth one.

Ironically, Mrs. Gandhi was selected by the party not because she was powerful, but because a syndicate of the party's leaders perceived her as powerless. General elections were only a year away, and Indira had the national appeal that they lacked. Her well-known face was to win the elections, and Indira was to be a puppet leader for a time while the actual struggle for power went on behind the scenes.

PRIME MINISTER

5

So it was that Indira Gandhi, almost accidentally, became the leader of the world's largest democracy. She had always claimed that she was not interested in power, and until now—she was nearing fifty—she had never actively pursued a position of power. Even as the struggle for prime minister was in progress, when it seemed possible that her arch rival, Morarji Desai, might win, Mrs. Gandhi kept a discreet silence, letting others canvass for her. The party bosses might not have been so sure of controlling this pensive, wistful woman who claimed she was not interested in being prime minister had they known what she was thinking. In a letter to her son Rajiv, she wrote that through it all, in her mind were the lines from a poem by Robert Frost, "How hard it is to keep from being king, when it's in you, and in the situation."

With very little formal political experience, India's youngest prime minister took office, assuring reporters that she felt "neither excited nor nervous," adding that being prime minister was "just another job I have to do."

It was her misfortune, however, that she took on the job at the worst time in India's postindependence history. The monsoon had failed for two consecutive years, threatening millions with starvation, adding yet another burden to an economy already depleted by two successive wars. The power structure had changed drastically since Nehru's years. The states were becoming more powerful, with each state fighting for it own interests. The Sikhs were demanding a separate state; the North and South were still at odds about Hindi being India's official language; and in the East, tribal revolts were proving difficult to contain. At the center, too, powerful party bosses controlled the Congress, and the prime minister was forced to compromise constantly with the various—often conflicting—power groups.

Internationally, India found itself almost completely isolated, its image at its lowest since independence. Within two years, India had been to war with both its neighbors, China and Pakistan; and the United States and England had tilted toward Pakistan in the latter conflict. The oil-rich Arab countries had openly supported Muslim Pakistan. The nonaligned movement, begun by Jawaharlal Nehru, had been discredited. To add to it all, the Soviet Union, always India's friend, seemed more interested now in maintaining a balance of power on the subcontinent than in promoting India.

Against these almost insurmountable odds, it is not surprising that Indira made little headway during her first year in office. In parliamentary debates, Mrs. Gandhi was unsure of herself, unable to take a firm stand, and often almost driven to tears as a result of constant heckling. She made it clear, however, that she was not afraid of controversy; she made two major decisions that year, both of them highly controversial. First, she divided the state of Punjab into two—Punjab and Haryana—thus giving in to Sikh demands for their own state, against established opinion of her own party. Second, in an effort to improve the foreign exchange situation, she devalued the Indian rupee. Although in the long run, neither of these steps helped solve intrinsic problems, they proved that the prime minister had the ability to make bold decisions, and the fortitude to stick them out in the face of fierce opposition.

It was in foreign relations, however, that Indira Gandhi appeared at her best. Used to meeting world leaders since she was a young girl, Indira managed to project her personality with a confidence and sparkle that charmed everyone; she received favorable coverage on her visits to America, England, and Russia, as well as to other, smaller countries.

In the 1967 elections, the Congress party was returned to power, but this time with a very narrow majority of only twenty-five seats in Parliament. The Congress had won every election to date, and it was used to victory. Its leaders had never even considered defeat. The opposition parties were—and remain to this day—regionally or community based, with little or no national image, and it seemed that the Congress had a monopoly of power. In this, the fifth general election, however, for the first time the Congress lost in eight states, and many of its most powerful leaders failed even to retain their seats. The near defeat of the Congress was a sure sign that the aging party leaders had become so involved with the power struggle at the center that they had lost touch with their electorate.

It was a jolt for the Congress, and it signaled a change in the Indian political style. India's years of idealism were over. The giants of the romantic freedom movement were dead or discredited—it was time for a younger group of leaders, and a more pragmatic approach to politics. Indira Gandhi symbolized both of these. She brought with her, also, the glamour of the Nehru name, a memory of a time when India seemed destined for greater things. And it was mainly because of Mrs. Gandhi that the Congress had managed to win the election. At the same time the campaign had given Mrs. Gandhi the confidence she needed to move forcefully into the role of prime minister.

A 1967 campaign billboard pictured Indira with her party's symbol, a pair of sacred bulls.

Mrs. Gandhi was not new to campaigning. But this was the first time that she had campaigned for herself, not for her father or her husband. Dressed in simple handspun saris, with her head demurely covered, she spoke plainly, explaining her position to the people with the help of simple metaphors and analogies. She had traveled tirelessly, to the remotest corners of the vast country, and wherever she went, she drew large crowds. The Congress party, however, had become very unpopular, and often she faced a hostile audience.

A challenge always drew out the best in Mrs. Gandhi. When she insisted on addressing a stormy public meeting in the state of Orissa, a stone thrown from the audience hit her on the nose, fracturing a bone. She won the admiration of her enemies when she refused to retire. Holding a blood-stained handkerchief to her nose, she went on with her speech, though the pain must have been excruciating. She continued the rest of her campaign with her nose and part of her face covered with bandages—an act that probably won her quite a few votes from the sentimental Indian public.

The elections taught her an important lesson, one that she never forgot: She realized that she could communicate with the Indian public far better than any of the other Congress leaders. She realized that she was the only one in the party with a national image, and that it was she who had won the elections for the Congress party. From this time onward, there was a marked change in her—for the first time, she began to pursue power. She had shown that she had a shrewd political insight, and with the Kerala ouster during her Congress presidency, she had indicated her gift for maneuvering and her disregard of the means to achieve her aims.

After the 1967 election, Mrs. Gandhi was no longer an interim prime minister, leading her country at the approval of her party bosses. She had now been elected by the people, and she pressed home her advantage immediately. In contrast to her former cabinet, chosen on the advice of the Congress leaders, this time Mrs. Gandhi chose her friends and confidants for all cabinet positions, admitting none of the followers of her rival, Morarji Desai. She was forced, however, to make Desai himself the deputy prime minister and to include him in her cabinet as finance minister. This gesture to the opposition, which must have irked her considerably, reflected the fact that the Syndicate—as the power group of older party bosses was now called—saw what was happening and was not willing to give up its power so easily. It was the members of this powerful group who had made Indira prime minister, and now that she was getting rebellious, they were convinced they could throw her out.

After two years of politicking, maneuvering, and bickering, the issue finally came to a head when Mrs. Gandhi openly rejected the Congress party nominee for president of India. In India, the president is a figurehead, elected by an electoral college, but he does have emergency powers in times of crisis. Mrs. Gandhi wanted to have someone sympathetic to her in that position. Knowing this, the Congress leaders proposed Sanjiva Reddy, a man who opposed the prime minister. Mrs. Gandhi put forward her own man, but when the Congress Parliamentary Board met on July 12, Reddy was elected as the Congress party nominee by a large majority.

It was a public humiliation, and an open threat to Mrs. Gandhi's leadership of her party. The prime minister hit back hard, and with lightening speed. On July 13, she persuaded V. V. Giri, the vice president, who had the backing of some opposition parties, to announce his intention of standing for president. On July 16, she wrote a letter to Desai, relieving him of his finance portfolio. She announced this to the press without waiting for Desai's reply. Mrs. Gandhi took over his finance portfolio, and within three days she nationalized the country's fourteen major banks, without waiting to consult the Parliament, which was to meet the next day.

The nationalization of banks was a purely political step, made against the judgment of the country's financial advisers. It was presented as a move that transferred capital to the people from the hands of large, private monopolies. The government promised easy loans to small farmers and businessmen, and though the bank bureaucracy was hardly prepared to deal with the change, the move was very popular with the people. Large crowds gathered outside Mrs. Gandhi's home every day, and she was draped with garlands of flowers, cheered, and hailed as a champion of the oppressed wherever she went.

It was exactly as Mrs. Gandhi had planned. Like a master chess player, she had conceived her moves far in advance and her opponents were caught at a disadvantage. They could not now oppose her nationalization of the banks, or object to the way in which she had dismissed Desai, because her actions now had a veneer of ideology. They were forced to bide their time. Mrs. Gandhi, however, pressed her advantage. She campaigned openly for presidential candidate V. V. Giri.

Members of the party, noting Mrs. Gandhi's popularity, realized the advantages of siding with her. Yet, since she was inciting Congress party members to vote against their own nominee, whose papers she herself had filed, proceedings took on a bizarre twist. "History does not record an instance where a Prime Minister, after proposing her party's candidate, not only works against him, but proclaims her support for the candidate of the opposition. If this tragic fact was not staring at us, I would have thought of it to be a tale from Alice in Wonderland," wrote the bewildered party president in an open letter to Indira Gandhi. On August 20, V. V. Giri was declared elected president of India; Indira had won the battle.

The war, however, was not over. Although the Syndicate was now in a weaker position, the struggle for power continued. This time, it was in the open. The twenty-one-member

Working Committee split neatly into two groups with ten members on each side. One member insisted on attending both of the meetings. Every day, the newspaper headlines screamed new accusations, and every day the capital was awash with rumors. Poor people demonstrated in favor of Mrs. Gandhi, convinced that she was fighting their cause.

Finally, on November 12, just over three months after Giri was elected president, the Syndicate formally expelled Indira Gandhi from the Indian National Congress, charging her with rebellion against the party. The official Congress Working Committee called upon the Congress parliamentary party to elect a new leader to replace the prime minister.

Mrs. Gandhi however, was not deterred. She had probably been awaiting the move to choose a new leader. With the support of 310 of the 429 Congress party members, Mrs. Gandhi announced that she had formed her own Congress party, henceforth to be called the Congress (R), the R standing for "ruling." The dejected members of the old guard, hanging on to the prestigious Congress name, called themselves the Congress (O): the O stood for "organization," but was always referred to as "old."

Mrs. Gandhi was now undisputed leader of the ruling party, but her troubles were not yet over. The Congress had come to power on a very narrow majority. With the split, the Congress (R) lost the majority, and the government became a sort of a coalition, with Mrs. Gandhi forced to depend upon the support of opposition parties to achieve a majority in the house. Instead of rushing into a midterm election at that time, Mrs. Gandhi decided to consolidate her position. Wanting to make up for losses resulting from the split, she encouraged defections from other parties, allowing everyone, regardless of reputation or ideology, to join the Congress (R).

During this time, she traveled widely throughout the country, feeling the mood of the Indian electorate. Then, toward the end of 1970, with her accurate sense of political timing, she dissolved Parliament before the end of its five-year term, and in January, 1971, announced elections to be held the following March.

Indira Gandhi was the center of the election campaign. Although Nehru, and later Indira, had been the primary performers in earlier election campaigns, never before had all attention been focused entirely on one leader. Four opposition parties formed an alliance aimed only at ousting her, and their platform consisted mainly of Mrs. Gandhi's misdeeds. The Congress (R) concentrated entirely on Indira. There were Indira badges and Indira posters, and it was Indira who campaigned for most of her nominees. From mid-January until the elections in March, she is said to have addressed 409 election meetings with a total attendance of twenty million people. She fed the people with populist phrases, convincing them that she stood for stability as well as social change. "Indira *hatao*" (remove Indira) shrilled the opposition; "*Garibi hatao*" (remove poverty) answered Indira, with a neat turn of phrase.

This time, the Congress (R) swept the polls, winning 350 seats in the 525-member lower house.

Mrs. Gandhi had spent the three years since the 1967 elections consolidating her position. Now, she had arrived. She had emerged as the undisputed leader of the ruling party, as well as of the country. Each new decision seems to have given her fresh confidence, so that now there remained almost nothing of the shy, unsure woman who had entered the arena less than a decade before. She had made the older leaders appear almost irrelevant. She had shown herself to be a brilliant tactician with an almost infallible sense of political timing, and she had instituted her own brand of politics. Now, riding the crest of the "Indira wave," she was free to rule her country almost as she wished.

Mrs. Gandhi's first task was to deal with her neighbor. With independence, the Indian subcontinent had been

Prime Minister Gandhi campaigned extensively
and effectively for the 1971 election, and
enthusiastic supporters like those shown here
gave her a resounding victory.

divided in two: secular India, with its Hindu majority, and Muslim Pakistan. Because the Muslim population was predominant in two very separate areas, Pakistan had been divided into West and East, with a large section of Northern India in the middle. In 1971, civil war broke out between the East and West Pakistans, and the dominant West Pakistani army moved into the East. The Pakistani civil war began to affect the Indian economy when thousands of refugees poured across the eastern border into the Indian state of Bengal. Ignoring advice to march troops into East Pakistan right away, Mrs. Gandhi opted instead to make the world aware of the problems. "One cannot but be perturbed when fire breaks out in a neighbor's house," was how she put it. She aimed at securing a peaceful settlement in East Pakistan through international pressure or, failing that, to prepare the ground for a military solution.

In the meantime, an unexpected détente had occurred between the United States and China, both allies of Pakistan. India was left in an isolated position on the subcontinent. The United States was supplying arms to Pakistan, and it seemed probable that they would, once again, side with Pakistan in the event of another war. It was against this background that Indira decided to sign a treaty with the Soviet Union. She had watched from the wings while India's earlier wars with China and Pakistan had been mishandled. This time, she was determined to prepare carefully.

A twenty-year Indo-Soviet Treaty of "Peace, Friendship, and Cooperation" between the two countries had been suggested by Moscow in 1969, but Mrs. Gandhi had declined, because she felt it would jeopardize India's relations with China and the United States. Now, however, it seemed necessary. The treaty included a statement of the Soviet Union's respect for India's nonalignment and provided for "mutual consultations" and appropriate effective measures to counter any military threat to either country. The treaty was a deviation from Indira's traditional stance of nonalignment, and it came under considerable criticism at home. ". . . it does not preclude us from signing similar treaties with other countries. . . . By signing it, we have not joined the Soviet Bloc," she assured the nation, and more pointedly, argued that the change in policy was a small price to pay for Soviet backing in the current crisis.

Mrs. Gandhi launched a massive campaign to bring her problem to the attention of the world. She wrote personally to twenty-four heads of state, and in October, she set out on a tour of Europe and America. On earlier visits Mrs. Gandhi's tone had been mild and noncontroversial. This time, she was sharp, direct, and uncompromising. Her stance reflected her new confidence in herself, as well as her confidence in the position into which she had maneuvered her country. "We are not dependent upon what other countries think or want us to do," she said in a BBC interview. "We know what we want for ourselves, and we are going to do it, whatever it costs. . . . We welcome help from any country; but if it doesn't come, well, its all right by us." Then, getting more aggressive, "When Hitler was on the rampage, why didn't you say, let's keep peace with Germany and let the Jews die, or let Belgium die, let France die?" she stormed, referring to the acts of genocide by the Pakistani army in the East. Her tour of Western Europe was a success. She charmed the leaders and the press, and she convinced them of the rightness of her cause.

In Washington, things were different. President Richard Nixon's administration had always tilted toward the military regime of Pakistan, and Nixon's meeting with Mrs. Gandhi made little difference to that position. The heads of the world's two largest democracies did not take to each other, and arms sales to Pakistan continued, despite Nixon's promise to put a stop to them. But Mrs. Gandhi had prepared her ground, and now she returned to India to wait. She supplied arms and training to the East Pakistani guerillas, but insisted constantly that she would be "the last person to start a war."

Provoked by the raids, Pakistan attacked India on December 3. President Yahya Khan of Pakistan had calculated upon immediate intervention of the superpowers and a UN freeze on the eastern border. Indira, however, had done her groundwork, and had planned her strategy well. In the West, India fought only a defensive battle, concentrating instead on the East. And although America voiced its support of Pakistan, and Russia, its support of India, the Indian army, fighting alongside East Pakistani guerilla fighters, secured a surrender from the West Pakistani army within fifteen days, before the superpowers had time to intervene.

Though the war lasted only fifteen days, it was a decisive one. Pakistan was now split into two nations; East Pakistan was renamed Bangladesh, and functioned as an independent country. India became, indisputably, the leading power on the subcontinent.

Mrs. Gandhi was at the peak of her power. She was mobbed and garlanded wherever she went, and, as they had done to the Mahatma, people touched her feet, addressing her as *ma* (Mother) or even *devi* (goddess). The seeds of Mrs. Gandhi's downfall, however, had already been sown. Her popularity created expectations that she could not fulfill. The cost of the war, a sharp rise in oil prices, and two years of successive drought had led the economy into a crisis. Prices soared, and the people began to raise their voices in protest. Neither Indira's tactical genius nor her charisma—the two qualities that had gotten her to this point—had equipped her to deal with the mammoth problems facing the vast, developing country. At this time, Mrs. Gandhi seemed satisfied to let events take their own course, concerning herself more with internal power politics than with the deteriorating conditions in the country.

Mrs. Gandhi met with Indian army
soldiers as tensions heated up
on the India/Pakistan border in
the early days of December 1971.

The Indian National Congress, when it expelled Mrs. Gandhi in 1969, had charged her with "constant denigration of the Congress organisation, [a] tendency to divide Congressmen among those who are her supporters and those who are not . . . [a] basic and over-riding desire to concentrate all power in her hands so that her colleagues are her nominees in any offices they might occupy."

These were, indeed, the tactics she had used to attain power, and she continued to use them, even when her position was secure. She did not trust anyone, and she let no one trust her completely. She hardly consulted her ministers, relying on friends, called her "kitchen cabinet," for advice. Her basic mistrust, however, was so deeply rooted that she would not allow any of these groups to remain for long, or to function unitedly. She incited rivalries in all groups, so that they were not allowed to perform at their best. This prevented anyone from rising to power, but, when it came to formulating or supplementing policies and programs, it served as a major setback. "She has surrounded herself with pygmies, and nobody can do a giant's job," said a politician who had once been her colleague.

By 1974, the situation was out of control. In the western, industrialized state of Gujarat, students led violent demonstrations against high prices, the opposition asked for a dissolution of the Congress assembly, and Morarji Desai, who still lingered in the political scene, went on an indefinite fast, turning the issue into a moral one. In his home state of Bihar, Jayaprakash Narayan, a venerated leader of the freedom struggle, led students in a similar protest, calling for a "total revolution," and union leader George Fernandez engineered a strike of the entire Indian railway system, crippling transport. Mrs. Gandhi's critics charged her with misuse of moral authority, corruption, and an erosion of moral leadership.

The press in India—there were at the time 835 newspapers and 13,925 magazines—was a free one, and now most of them were vociferous in their criticism of the prime minister. Since it is not easy to sue for defamation in India, the press and Mrs. Gandhi's critics often resorted to pure slander. Just as she was elevated to the position of *devi* [goddess] after the Bangladesh war, she was now held responsible for everything that was wrong in the country. Although it was impossible for any government to solve all the nation's ills, Mrs. Gandhi's style of leadership did not help matters much.

One of the most penetrating criticisms of Mrs. Gandhi came from G. B. Verghese, widely respected editor of the *Hindustan Times.* "The Prime Minister has no program, no world view, no grand design," he said in 1974. "Thus, bereft of a frame, she has largely reacted to events and failed to shape them. This has been her tragedy. She lacks economic and administrative expertise. Nevertheless, she has a certain political instinct and charisma which would have been the greater assets if harnessed to a greater purpose. She has a mandate but no mission."

EMERGENCY

6

In August 1972, when Indira Gandhi was at the peak of her power, she was asked to list India's main achievements since independence. "I would say our greatest achievement is to have survived as a free and democratic nation," she answered.

On June 26, 1975, through a presidential proclamation, Mrs. Gandhi declared a state of emergency in India. For the first time since independence, she imposed total press censorship and suspended civil liberties guaranteed by the constitution—including freedom of expression and association and the right to appeal to the courts against arbitrary arrest. "In India democracy has given too much license to the people," she said. "Sometimes bitter medicine has to be administered to a patient to cure him."

The crisis began with the decision of a high court judge in Mrs. Gandhi's native Allahabad, convicting her on two rather minor counts of electoral corruption—using government officials and government jeeps for her campaign. The judgment annulled her election to Parliament and barred her from public office for six years.

Mrs. Gandhi appealed to the Supreme Court, the highest court of appeal in India. Opposition parties, already vociferous in their criticism of her, demanded her immediate resignation. For the first time, they saw the possibility of obtaining power; they organized rallies and demonstrations and gave impassioned speeches all over the country, demanding that Mrs. Gandhi respect the judgment of the court, and step down immediately.

It is reported that on the day of the judgment, Mrs. Gandhi did consider stepping down, and it was her younger son Sanjay who stopped her. He convinced her that if she gave up her position now, she would never get it back. In answer to opposition rallies, Sanjay, with the help of city officials, organized demonstrations and meetings in support of his mother, so that New Delhi soon began to resemble a circus.

Meanwhile, in those days of hysteria, Mrs. Gandhi had two options open to her. She could respect the judgment of the court and step down for a while, until the Supreme Court judgment was announced, giving the position of prime minister to a loyal member of her cabinet. The second option was to keep her power by force, and this is what she chose to do. A member of her cabinet said later in an interview, "In the Upanishads [Hindu Scriptures] they say there are always two paths, and there is always a moment of choice. Her not resigning led to everything that happened thereafter."

For the first time, Mrs. Gandhi saw the possibility of power being snatched away from her, and she became almost paranoiac in her defiance of the mounting opposition. She said she had suffered lies and abuse in the interest of the common man. It was not a question of choosing Indira Gandhi or the Congress, she said, it was her "duty to serve the people."

Mrs. Gandhi realized, however, that she could not remain in office under the present circumstances, and so she

In response to mounting political opposition
and demonstrations calling for
her resignation, Prime Minister Gandhi
declared a national state of emergency
on June 26, 1975, suspending civil liberties
and jailing hundreds of her political opponents.

turned to the "emergency" measures provided in the Constitution of India. The constitution allows for these "emergency" measures under a severe threat to the country, such as war. Claiming now that the opposition had subverted democracy, and that India was threatened with anarchy, Mrs. Gandhi declared a state of emergency in her country.

At 4:00 P.M. on June 25, Mrs. Gandhi had decided to impose the emergency, but she did not confide this to any of the members of her cabinet. At six-thirty that evening, her aides began to telephone the homes of chief ministers of states all over the country. They were informed that everyone in the opposition must be jailed, but without the knowledge of the press. Police went to newspaper offices, cutting off electrical supplies, and, in some cases, destroying the proofs of the stories already filed so that there would be no papers in the morning. Except for a few top officers, neither the police nor members of the administration were aware of the reasons for their actions. It was only at 11:20 P.M. that the president of India signed the draft proclamation prepared at the prime minister's residence, and the emergency came into effect. The members of her cabinet still did not know of the emergency. At 6:00 A.M. she called a meeting at her residence. In keeping with her usual style, she did not explain, and she did not ask for opinions. It took her less than fifteen minutes to inform her ministers that she had imposed an emergency and arrested hundreds of opposition leaders, including Morarji Desai and Jayaprakash Narayan.

Mrs. Gandhi announced to her people that the emergency was a response to the threat to internal security and assured them that it was only temporary. She announced a new twenty-point program that she said was designed to bring down prices and initiate agrarian reform. She pointed out that everything she did was perfectly constitutional. Her Congress party had a majority in the Parliament, and they ratified the emergency. Amendments to the Maintenance of

Internal Security Act (MISA) expanded her powers and allowed the government to seize the property of people who were detained, or went into hiding. In less than two months, over five thousand people were said to have been jailed.

On November 5, the Supreme Court dismissed the charges against Mrs. Gandhi. The ruling was based on a rewritten election law passed after her conviction in June that omitted the offenses of which she had been found guilty. Now that she was "free," people hoped that she would lift the emergency. Instead, she announced only a month later that the elections scheduled for 1976 would be postponed for a year. India, like most of the countries that surrounded it, was now a totalitarian state, and Indira Gandhi was its dictator.

It was in those years that Indira's son, Sanjay Gandhi, gained importance. Born on December 14, 1946, he was the younger of her two sons, and her favorite. Sanjay, who had served as a Rolls Royce apprentice in London, was professedly unacademic. He had a penchant for girls and a passion for cars. Unlike Indira's older son, Rajiv—a quiet, unassuming airline pilot who preferred to call himself Captain Rajiv, rather than use the Gandhi name—Sanjay had already acquired a shady reputation and a flamboyant style.

He entered politics from the top, and his initiation was immediate. Even before the emergency, he had begun to deal with state ministers on national issues. On June 25, when the emergency was being debated at the prime minister's home, he advised that high courts and newspaper offices be forcibly closed. He gathered around him a group of toughs and flatterers and diverted most of his energies to his two favorite programs—mass sterilization as a means of achieving population control, and destruction and "relocation" of the shantytowns that had grown up around Delhi.

Indira, too, had acquired power from her father, but she had been discreet at first and was careful to keep a low profile. Also, as prime minister she had scrupulously avoided even a hint of a scandal in her personal life, knowing that in a society as traditional as India, even a second marriage would mean political suicide.

"Sanjay in politics," says Uma Vasudev, author of *Two Faces of Indira Gandhi*, "was like a bull in a china shop." He had no patience with the tactical maneuvering that was his mother's forte. He believed in the politics of confrontation, and he bullied and badgered his way into the center of the stage, while his doting mother looked on.

Soon, he and his group began to be associated with the worst of the excesses of the emergency. He was held responsible for the dreaded forced sterilizations that had become party policy, for the imprisonment and torture of anyone who opposed him, and for the senseless destruction of people and property.

People who had known Indira for a long time assumed that she was unaware of her son's excesses. They explained his growing influence over her, and her silence at his Mafia-like tactics, as the devotion of a lonely, isolated woman for a favorite son. "Those who attack Sanjay" she said, "attack me," adding that her son was one of the few people she could really trust. But her critics maintain that she was too sharp, and too shrewd a politician, to be unaware of Sanjay's controversial actions. They said that she used him as a sort of "test pilot" to pursue policies that she was afraid to associate with herself. "Rightly or wrongly" wrote author Ved Mehta in *A Family Affair*, "Sanjay was seen as representing the ruthless side of his mother."

Opposition parties claimed that India had entered an era of darkness, and, as the atrocities of the emergency continued, they seemed to lose hope that the country would ever emerge. Then, without a warning, in January 1977 Indira Gandhi announced that elections would be held in March of that year, because of her "unshakable faith in the power of the people."

Outwardly, the emergency rule had improved conditions in the country. Fear of strong reprisals had resulted in stricter discipline, and higher production in India's large, bureaucratic public sector. Strikes had been outlawed, and the economy seemed to be functioning smoothly. A large loan from the International Monetary Fund, coupled with a good monsoon, had stabilized prices of essential commodities. Indira Gandhi was convinced that she would win, and her intelligence reports confirmed her opinions.

No leader in the world has voluntarily stepped down after a period of authoritarian rule and allowed the country to go to the polls. Dictators such as Pakistan's Zia-ul-Huq have, under pressure from the West, held elections, but they have been rigged. Indira Gandhi had been receiving adverse publicity abroad, and she probably saw this as a way of getting a sanction for her style. Both she and her father had always won every election they had stood for, and she probably believed that the people would always be behind her. No doubt, she decided to hold elections because she believed she would win. But it was a brave decision, one of the biggest risks of her career, and cannot be so easily explained. She had grown up under men like Nehru and Gandhi, men who held democracy as sacred, and perhaps she was moved to call elections because she was not entirely comfortable with her image as a dictator.

Mrs. Gandhi released opposition members from prison, lifted press censorship, and began to campaign. With only two months before the election, the opposition was in shambles and Mrs. Gandhi was sure they would never be able to challenge the organized might of the Congress, loaded as it was with obedient workers and with funds. Indira's own constituency of Rai Bareilly, a rather remote area of the populous state of Uttar Pradesh, had usually given her a comfortable majority. Now she got her son Sanjay to stand from the adjoining constituency of Amethi.

However, she had underestimated the opposition, as

well as the extent of public opinion against her regime. United by the privations suffered in jail, the opposition, for the first time in Indian history, gathered under one banner. They called themselves the Janata party, the "party of the people." There was a revolt within her own party as well. Jagjivan Ram, a cabinet member known as the "iron man," whom she had not been able to get rid of but whose power she had consistently undermined during the emergency, left her party, along with a group of dissidents, and joined the Janata.

The Janata was short of funds and lacking in organization, but its rallies drew large, cheering crowds. Businessmen were willing to back them, and even the poorer people poured money into their coffers. The short election campaign soon turned into a people's movement that echoed the country's freedom struggle.

It seemed that Indira Gandhi had become a prisoner of her own propaganda. Having dismissed everyone who showed signs of independence from her party, she was surrounded now by sycophants, and had, according to biographer Zareer Masani, "deluded herself into the belief that her own leadership, followed by her son's, was synonymous with the well-being of the country."

"India is Indira, Indira is India," one of her colleagues had said during the emergency, and it is possible that she had begun to believe this herself.

As in 1971, the entire election centered around Indira Gandhi. The opposition promised a relief from her regime, and her own party had only one performer—herself. Mrs. Gandhi did her best. Although suffering from facial herpes— a painful inflammation of nerve endings—she stuck to a rigorous campaign schedule. But this time her rallies were poorly attended, and her audiences often hostile. She pointed in vain to the economic gains made during the emergency, she denied knowledge of any excesses, and she insisted on defending her son. In a desperate attempt to regain the sympathy of the public, she claimed that the opposition was planning to assassinate her and her family, but no one believed her.

It was obvious that the people had turned against Indira Gandhi. And, toward the end of her campaign, she must have known that she would not win. People wondered if she would cancel the elections, clamp the opposition into jail again, and muzzle the press. But Indira had never been one to run away from a challenge, and she stood her ground. She probably realized, too, that she could not indefinitely control a country like India without its consent.

When the votes were counted, the Congress party was routed, and both Indira Gandhi and her son even lost their seats in Parliament. In a desperate attempt to keep the people unaware of the election results, the state-owned radio and television refused to announce the Gandhis' defeat, constantly telling the audience only of the few seats that the Congress had won. Because of this, there were widespread rumors that Indira had planned a military takeover, but that the service chiefs had refused to comply.

Mrs. Gandhi finally stepped down gracefully, and for the first time since Indian independence, a non-Congress government came into power.

"I could have become an interior decorator. I could have become a dancer. . . ." Indira had said once, indicating that politics was not the only path open to her. But now, defeated at the polls at age sixty, Mrs. Gandhi showed no inclination to retire, and there was no sign that she wanted to do anything but continue in politics.

Members of the Congress, however, felt that she was too much of a liability, and were maneuvering to drop her when Mrs. Gandhi, for the second time, split her party. This time, there were no pretenses. Her party was called Con-

*Supporters greeted the former prime minister
with flowers upon her release from
jail a week after her arrest on charges
that she had violated the constitution
during the state of emergency.*

gress (I), where the *I* stood for "Indira." She won a by-election from a rural district in South India in early 1978, and was back in the Parliament.

Meanwhile, the Janata Party, headed by her old rival Morarji Desai—now way past seventy—had restored democracy, veered toward the United States in its foreign policy, and set up a commission to investigate Indira Gandhi's role in the emergency excesses. She was arrested twice, and when she refused bail, she was jailed for a few days, then released for lack of sufficient evidence.

The Janata Party was a coalition made up of small parties with differing ideologies and led by old men who had waited almost a lifetime to lead the country. Now, they fell to quarreling among themselves.

This was Indira's forte. Now she began to campaign actively, and to complain against the ineffectual, weak government at the center. She waited for the infighting to intensify. She encouraged an aging Charan Singh, a man she had earlier imprisoned, to leave the Janata with his followers, promising him the support of her Congress (I).

Morarji Desai was forced to resign in July 1979, and Singh became the leader of the new government. Mrs. Gandhi waited for the split in the Janata to become final, and then she withdrew her support from Charan Singh, who lost his majority in the Parliament. Once again, the country had to go to the polls.

Indira campaigned actively. The Janata Party had split into smaller factions, and the people, disenchanted with its bungling, swept Indira back into power, giving the Congress (I) a two-thirds majority in the Parliament.

The emergency and the short Janata rule, however, form an extremely important period in Indian history. It was the first definite indication that the Indian electorate, mostly illiterate and living in isolated villages, was aware of its rights and conscious of its political freedom.

THE
SECOND
REIGN

7

The people had forgiven Mrs. Gandhi her excesses, and they were willing to have her rule again. They had tried the opposition, and found them wanting. India, it appeared, had no alternative but Indira Gandhi.

"Maybe [the Janata Party] made Government policy, but I was at the center of Indian politics. I was the main issue of discussion at every Cabinet meeting," said Indira Gandhi to an interviewer just before her reelection. And, when her party was swept back into power, she said that victory had been won "entirely on my name." She could have ruled her country, secure in the knowledge that India really needed her.

Instead, her victory signaled a major change in Mrs. Gandhi's style. Back in power, she now seemed afraid—sometimes almost paranoid—of losing it again. She had seen the way people had deserted her during her downfall, and now loyalty became the only criterion for holding office. She even freed two young men who had hijacked a plane to protest her being jailed and gave them seats in the state legislature. Always suspicious of leaders with a power base of

*Indira, newly returned to power,
with favored son Sanjay*

their own, Mrs. Gandhi continued to surround herself with sycophants. Her new cabinet was considered to be the weakest in the country's history, and in the states run by the Congress (I), the chief ministers dared not make a move without consulting the prime minister. She was firmly entrenched in her post, she had evolved her own style of leadership, she had the sanction of her people, and she probably expected the years ahead to be smooth ones.

The last years of her life, however, were among the stormiest in her checkered career, and in the history of the country that she ruled. Barely six months after her victory, her notorious son Sanjay—now a member of Parliament, and her heir apparent—was killed attempting a daredevil stunt in a small plane above New Delhi. He was thirty-four years old, and his death devastated Mrs. Gandhi. Although her iron reserve did not crack in public, she became withdrawn and distracted, showing little interest in public matters. She emerged from this period of mourning, however, more determined than ever to create a Nehru-Gandhi dynasty. Her elder son Rajiv was now brought into the forefront.

Up to this time, Rajiv, age thirty-six, had shunned all publicity. He had appeared to be his brother's opposite—a shy, soft-spoken, slightly chubby airline pilot who had no political ambitions whatsoever. With his Italian-born wife Sonia, and his two children, he had lived in the same house as Mrs. Gandhi and Sanjay, but he had managed to stay out of all controversy. After Sanjay's death, however, he reluctantly accepted his political legacy only, he said, to "help Mummy." In June 1981, he stood for a by-election in Uttar Pradesh and won his brother's seat in Parliament, as well as Sanjay's place on the executive committee of the Congress (I) youth wing.

But the war of succession had just begun. Sanjay's young widow Menaka—a onetime model whose pictures, in which she was draped in nothing but a towel, had been hurriedly withdrawn from magazines when she won Sanjay's hand—did not relish losing the limelight. During the emergency and after, the impulsive and high-spirited Menaka had attracted as much controversy as her husband. Now, after his death, she wished to continue in his stead.

Predictably, Mrs. Gandhi chose her reluctant son instead, and the rebellious Menaka, along with her baby son Feroze Varuh, was thrown out of the house that she had shared with her mother-in-law. Menaka, however, had learned her politics from her mother-in-law, and she was not to be cowed. She formed her own party, the Rashtriya Sanjay Vichar Manch (the National Sanjay Platform), and pitted herself against her brother-in-law from her husband's constituency of Amethi. She attracted large, curious crowds as she visited areas of discontent, holding forth against the ruling party dressed always in simple, elegant cotton saris like her mother-in-law. Mrs. Gandhi might have ignored Menaka's outburst, thus allowing it to die a natural death. Instead, she raised hysterical allegations against her daughter-in-law and played directly into Menaka's hand, a move that was entirely uncharacteristic of the prime minister.

In the years to come, there were other indications that Mrs. Gandhi's famous political instinct was finally leaving her. Early in 1983, Mrs. Gandhi risked holding elections in the troubled northeastern state of Assam. Refugees from neighboring East Pakistan, now Bangladesh, had been streaming into Assam even before Mrs. Gandhi took office. The creation of the independent nation of Bangladesh had been, among other things, an attempt at solving the refugee problem. Muslims from the troubled and poverty-stricken Bangladesh, however, continued to pour into Assam, creating severe shortages and much resentment in the state. The threatened residents of Assam had been agitating for a separate status for the refugees, called "foreigners." The government, however, had made them citizens, even allowing them the right to vote. Tensions between the refugees and the original residents reached a peak in 1983. In this context, Mrs. Gandhi risked holding state elections, including the "foreigners" in the electoral rolls. As a result, on the eve of the election, the hostilities exploded in a riot in which more than four thousand people were killed.

More trouble lay ahead in India's northernmost state, Kashmir. Set amidst the Himalayan mountains, Kashmir is one of India's most beautiful states, and one of its most troubled. Strategically situated between China and Pakistan, Kashmir has been the scene of intense military activity in all of India's wars. Border areas disputed by Pakistan and China lie within this troubled state. It was also, until 1984, one of the few Indian states not ruled by Indira Gandhi's Congress (I) party.

Not willing to admit defeat, Mrs. Gandhi tried the tactics she had first used in Kerala, when she was Congress party president. The state Congress (I) party led agitations and demonstrations that often turned violent, making a case for dismissal of the ruling government on the grounds that it could no longer maintain law and order.

Soon after, Mrs. Gandhi tried the same tactics in the southern state of Andhra Pradesh. This time, however, she had underestimated the popularity of her rival, Chief Minister N. T. Rama Rao. An aging film idol who was almost unknown outside his state, Rao—popularly known as NTR—formed his own political party, crisscrossed the state in a converted caravan, and swept the polls in a decisive victory in the state elections held in 1983.

Attempts by the state Congress (I) party to unseat Rao as the state's chief minister failed in 1984, and sparked a nationwide protest against the Congress (I) tactics. Realizing that she had tarnished her image, Mrs. Gandhi denied knowledge of the incident—it was an internal state matter, she said—but not even her supporters could believe her.

It was also in 1984 that Mrs. Gandhi faced the most difficult challenge of her career, this time in the state of Punjab. Known as the "breadbasket" of India, Punjab is the richest state in the country, largely due to the perseverance and hard work of the Sikhs, who make up around 52 percent of its population.

The Akali Dal, the state-based Sikh party, had been agitating for greater autonomy for its state for four years, but the government had paid little heed to its demands. One reason was Indira's usual suspicion of parties with a local power base. Another reason was the justified fear that granting more autonomy to Punjab would set a precedent that would lead other states to make similar demands. In a country like India, where each state has a separate identity, such demands would lead, eventually, to the disintegration of the nation.

In order to cut the power of the Akali Dal, Mrs. Gandhi resorted to her usual tactics—she encouraged another power group as a rival. Sanjay Gandhi is reported to have contributed funds to Sant Jarnail Singh Bhindranwale as early as 1977, when he was a little-known fundamentalist leader. But Bhindranwale soon became too powerful for Indira Gandhi.

Sporting a black leather bandoleer with polished silver bullets, the young preacher with his flashing black eyes and his fiery exhortations for a return to the fundamentals of the Sikh religion struck a responsive chord in young Sikhs in search of romance. Soon, as the head of a vast following, he began to demand complete independence from India; he began to agitate for a new Sikh nation, called Khalistan.

The Akalis, led by Harchand Singh Longowal, soon came to be known as moderates, who favored negotiations instead of Bhindranwale's violence. Still, Indira stalled. Negotiating with the Sikhs, she felt, would be seen as a show of weakness among the Hindus of the state.

Bhindranwale and his group, however, grew increasingly

violent, killing and terrorizing the surrounding area. By early 1984, Hindu resistance to their attacks increased, and the violence reached alarming levels. After two years of escalating violence, Mrs. Gandhi finally agreed to negotiate with the Akali Dal. The terrorists, by this time, were in no mood to accept any conciliation reached by their rival group. They had converted their oldest shrine, the Golden Temple, into a heavily armed fortress, in which they lived side by side with visiting pilgrims. Even as preparations for talks were under way, they gunned down a respected writer and Congress (I) member, V. N. Tiwari, and they threatened to kill one more public official every day.

Declaring Punjab to be "dangerously disturbed," Mrs. Gandhi stationed paramilitary forces in the state and gave security forces broad powers of arrest and detention. Then, on June 1, the militants of the Golden Temple opened fire on the paramilitary forces surrounding the complex, killing eleven of them in one shooting spree.

"The time for talking with terrorists has run out," announced an exasperated Mrs. Gandhi. On June 5, fifteen thousand troops moved into Punjab, fifty-four hundred of them stationed around the seventy-two acre complex of the Golden Temple. Pilgrims were asked to leave the temple, journalists and photographers were ordered out of the state, and transport and communication lines were cut. Punjab was sealed from the rest of the world as the army opened fire on the Golden Temple.

The militants, however, were far better organized and equipped than the army had bargained for. The army, which had envisaged using only bayonets, was forced to use tanks and artillery to counter the sophisticated weapons—including antitank missiles, rockets, and mortars—used by the Sikh militants. At least six hundred people, including Bhindranwale, who had sworn not to be taken alive, were killed in the fray, and the temple was flushed out. Although her critics

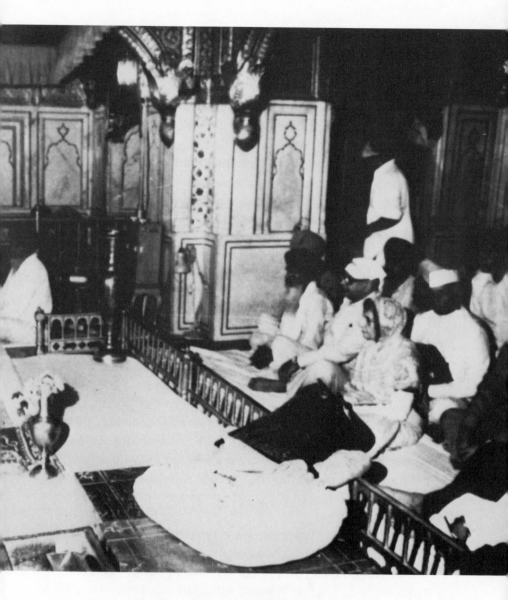

Mrs. Gandhi at a prayer meeting inside the Golden Temple a few weeks after the army assault flushed out Sikh rebels who had turned the temple into a terrorist fortress

claimed that she had stalled too long, in the end the decision had been inevitable, and it won Mrs. Gandhi the admiration of many of her countrymen. Sikh militants, however, swore revenge. They vowed to kill her, and on October 31, 1984, they succeeded.

"Mrs. Gandhi was the most remarkable woman I have ever met," says well-known Indian journalist Dom Moraes. "You never recovered from her sting, but it was equally hard to recover from her smile."

She had about her a grace and dignity, and an almost regal manner, the kind that made people stand up straighter when she entered a room. People meeting her for the first time, and prepared to dislike her, often found themselves charmed by her soft voice and by the smile that broke out suddenly, lighting up her eyes.

She was always elegant—even after a long, hot day on the road—and she took trouble with her appearance. Her nails were always manicured, her eyebrows always neatly plucked, and she usually kept a freshly ironed sari at hand on journeys, changing just before arrival.

Almost nothing is known about her personal life. Mrs. Gandhi gave many interviews, but she rarely relaxed, and she never revealed herself. Any personal questions were usually met with an icy silence. She was at her best at the large, packed campaign rallies that were a hallmark of her career, and she admitted that campaigning buoyed her. Wherever she went, people would garland her, touch her feet, and call her *ma*, or mother.

It is difficult to explain her hold on the Indian public. Even her critics were forced to admit that India had no alternative but Indira Gandhi. The opposition, made up mostly of tired old men who had been forced to leave the Congress because Indira no longer wanted them, was no match for her. Thirty-seven years after independence, India has no party to rival the Congress with a comprehensive platform, and no leader with a nationwide appeal. It is true that Indira Gandhi did not allow anyone to grow within her Congress party, but even the opposition could not throw up a leader to match her stature. In her lifetime, Indira Gandhi reigned supreme.

"After an idealist like Nehru, India needed a pragmatist, like his daughter, as a leader," wrote Moraes just after her death, and there is no doubt that the long father-daughter rule has benefited India in many ways.

Foremost among them is India's foreign policy. Nehru believed in nonalignment. He was fiercely anticolonial, and saw an alignment with either the Soviet or the U.S. bloc merely as another form of colonialism. His daughter Indira continued with this policy, in spite of fierce criticism from the United States, which saw India's refusal to toe the line as a sign of rebellion, especially in light of the foreign aid that the United States supplied to India.

In 1971, however, Indira Gandhi signed the Indo-Soviet Friendship Treaty, for the first time linking India's security with the foreign policy objectives of another nation. The treaty, prompted in part by continued U.S. arms aid to Pakistan on the eve of India's war with that country, is definitely seen as a tilt toward the Soviet bloc. As a result, much to American chagrin, India termed the 1979 Soviet invasion of Afghanistan "an internal matter."

India, however, is far from being a "Soviet proxy." It follows its own foreign policy. It refused, for example, to sign the Nuclear Non-Proliferation Treaty, in spite of pressure tactics applied by both the superpowers. And India exploded its own nuclear device, knowing that both the superpowers would be critical of it. "I am neither pro-Russian, nor pro-American, only pro-Indian," said Mrs. Gandhi, irritable at the insistence that all Third World nations must belong to one of the two camps.

Under Indira Gandhi, India's economic policy went hand in hand with its foreign policy. It discouraged investment in India by multinational corporations, which Nehru felt represented another form of colonialism, and insisted on import restrictions that protected its own industry. This policy, forged by Nehru and followed by Indira, also came under intense criticism both abroad and at home, especially because of the substandard quality of goods India initially produced.

In the long run, however, the policy has paid off. India has among the largest technological bases in the world today. It ranks thirteenth in industrial output, and it has the third largest number of trained scientists. It is largely due to its economic policy that India is one of the only Third World nations that has the power to produce almost everything it needs—from cars to paper clips.

The combination of Nehru's idealism and Mrs. Gandhi's pragmatism has placed the country, says *The New York Times*, "among the world's most influential nations."

INDIA
WITHOUT
INDIRA

8

On the day of her death, Indira Gandhi's dearest wish was fulfilled—her son, Rajiv Gandhi, succeeded her as prime minister of India, continuing for the third generation the Nehru-Gandhi dynasty. It appeared as if Indira, the supreme tactician, had maneuvered the time and the manner of her own death so that, with her passing, the orphaned Congress (I) party had no choice but to elect her son as their new leader.

No one who has lived through the turbulent politics of Mrs. Gandhi's years as prime minister can deny her profound impact on the politics of the nation and of the subcontinent. No one who knew her can fail to admire her determination and her grit, and her profound understanding of the politics of survival. It is clear that Mrs. Gandhi saw politics primarily as an exercise in power. She destroyed anyone who dared to create a power base of his own, and, in doing so, she destroyed the democratic fabric of the Congress party, so carefully crafted a generation ago by her father and the leaders of the freedom struggle. Thus, elected officials gave way to appointed officials, within both the government and the

party, and the people in positions of power owed their rise to a moment of recognition by Indira Gandhi. And so, her passing created a dangerous power vacuum. The Congress party lost the single factor that held it together, and the opposition parties lost the centerpiece of their tactical calculations. With her death, the party had no time to prepare a successor. The country was erupting into violence, and the Congress (I) had only one person with a national image, only one man whose presence could steer the nation back to sanity—Rajiv Gandhi. Indira had never allowed anyone near her except her sons. Just as it seemed that while she lived, India had no alternative but Indira Gandhi, now, with her death, it seemed that it had no alternative but her son.

Almost nothing is known about Rajiv Gandhi—except that he has shunned politics for most of his forty years. Forced to enter the arena on the death of his younger brother four years ago, the westernized, soft-spoken elder son of Indira Gandhi had yet to make an impact on Indian politics when he was thrust suddenly into the limelight.

"Indira Gandhi was a mother not only to me, but to the entire nation," he said on his first public address to the nation, appealing for peace and restraint even as anti-Sikh riots flared across the nation. The violence subsided within a week, the country returned to normal, and, as soon as the official twelve-day period of mourning ended, India's youngest prime minister announced a general election, to be held in the last days of December.

Indira with her son Rajiv in the garden of her residence, on October 12, 1984. In the national elections held immediately after Indira Gandhi's assassination, Rajiv emerged as a forceful political leader and was swept into power largely on his own merits, not simply by birthright.

The five-year term of the *Lok Sabha* (House of Commons) was drawing to a close, and preparations for India's eighth general elections were under way even before Mrs. Gandhi's death. Amidst the hectic sloganizing and speech making that accompany an Indian campaign, newspapers and opinion polls predicted that Mrs. Gandhi was losing her hold over the nation and that she would return to power with a very slender majority—or worse, be forced to head a coalition government.

Announcing the date of elections is the prerogative of the ruling party. The Congress (I) scheduled the elections immediately after Mrs. Gandhi's assassination, hoping to ride into power on the sympathy wave that followed her death. The party was still called Congress (I) for Indira, and her face stared down from the election posters and banners that lined the streets. The Congress party had hoped to win the elections on Mrs. Gandhi's name. Her son was to keep a low profile, stressing mainly the martyrdom of his beloved mother.

But, as the campaign gathered momentum, it became clear that this time, Mrs. Gandhi would not win the elections for her party. Gradually, it was seen that it was not Indira, but Rajiv, who was the star performer of the election campaign. Dressed in a white *kurta payjama* (an informal Indian dress), the good-looking son of Mrs. Gandhi attracted mammoth crowds wherever he went. Soon, he stopped talking about his mother and began to tell the people what he would do for the country. He promised to rid India of poverty, corruption, and factionalism, to give the country a strong, united government. He was not saying anything that his mother had not said, or anything that was different from the campaign promises of the hordes of opposition politicians. But it was clear that the people were prepared to believe him.

In a country riddled with tired old politicians with corrupt track records, Rajiv's fresh young face was a welcome change. He projected a pleasing image, and he had one major advantage over his rivals—he had no past. And so, although it was impossible to predict what kind of leadership he had to offer, the people were prepared to give him a chance.

And so it was not Indira Gandhi, but her son, who won the elections for the Congress (I) party with the largest majority in India's history. And it was not a vote for sympathy, as the political pundits had originally predicted, but a vote for hope, that swept Rajiv into power. The people, tired of all existing politicians, declared that an 'unknown evil' was better than a known one. With three successive generations of Nehrus at the helm, India is now a "democratic monarchy," and Rajiv inherits the magic of the Nehru name. He inherits also the problems of poverty, overcrowding, and communal tension—all the seemingly insoluble problems that his mother wrestled with for most of her political career. One of Rajiv's first acts in office was to rid the ruling party of most of his mother's "yes men." He replaced them with dynamic young executives, intent upon ushering India into the twenty-first century. And now, with almost no political experience, Rajiv and his computer boys—as they are popularly called—face the formidable task of governing the most difficult country in the world.

Although it is too early to predict whether he will survive the quagmire of Indian politics, it is already apparent that Rajiv means to make many changes in his mother's policies. It is apparent, too, that the people are ready to forget Indira and enter the new era.

For many years it had appeared that India had no alternative but Indira Gandhi. It had appeared almost as if Indira and India were inseparable. And, though the legacy of her long and stormy career will be debated for years to come, now, barely a year after her death, Indira seems almost forgotten. Although it appears to be a fickle reaction from a people who, only a short time ago were mesmerized by her, it proves only that in a country as complex and resilient as India, it is difficult for any one person to make a lasting impression.

FOR FURTHER READING

Bhatia, Krishan. *Indira: A Biography of Prime Minister Gandhi.* New York: Angus & Robertson, 1974.

Brecher, Michael. *Political Leadership in India.* New Delhi: Vikas Publishing House, 1983.

Carras, Mary C. *Indira Gandhi in the Crucible of Leadership.* Bombay: Jaico Press, 1980.

Gandhi, Indira. *My Truth.* New York: Grove Press, 1980.

Hangen, Welles. *After Nehru, Who?* New York: Harcourt Brace & World, 1963.

Masani, Zareer. *Indira Gandhi, A Biography.* New Delhi: Oxford University Press, 1981.

Mellor, John W., ed. *India: A Rising Middle Power.* New Delhi: Westview Press, 1981.

Shouri, Arun. *Mrs. Gandhi's Second Reign.* New York: Advent, 1984.

Vasudev, Uma. *Two Faces of Indira Gandhi.* New Delhi: Vikas Publishing House, 1977.

Watson, Francis. *A Concise History of India.* London: Thames and Hudson, 1979.

INDEX